Let's Get Visible!

Get Brand Clarity, Stand Out in Your Industry
and Supercharge Your Business Growth

Sapna Pieroux

First published in Great Britain in 2019
by Rethink Press (www.rethinkpress.com)

Cover design by Sapna Pieroux 2019

DoSaySee model © InnerVisions ID 2018

The VISION Process™ InnerVisions ID 2019

Praise

'Let's Get Visible! *is a great read for any entrepreneur who wants to know more about branding and how it can boost their business success. As someone who has worked with thousands of entrepreneurs and built several businesses, I know how much of a difference branding makes to a business as it scales.*

I have personally witnessed the results of Sapna's VISION process with several of my own clients and the difference it makes to their confidence, the transformation it brings to their business is amazing. VISION is an innovative way to create the brand of your dreams as a collaboration with entrepreneur and designer.

If you want to create branding that will help you stand out and scale up, then this book is absolutely brilliant.'

Daniel Priestley, entrepreneur, author, speaker

'*Clarity, confidence and power. The VISION process is a journey with spectacular results: my business crystallised and took a form beyond what I ever could have imagined. So much of branding is not understood. Sapna gives all her clients – and now her readers – understanding, insight and true clarity. Funny, sharp and forward-thinking,* Let's Get Visible! *is a must-read for all business owners, new and established.'*

Lorna Reeves, founder and owner of MyOhMy Weddings and MyOhMy Events, Wedding Planner of the Year 2019

'Sapna provides an invaluable insight into the power of your company's branding. Packed with practical advice, actionable steps, case studies and a brilliant methodology to help you discover and implement branding that truly represents your values and speaks to your target market, this book is a must-read for any entrepreneur or business owner who wants to build a solid foundation for their brand. Sapna's writing style is engaging, witty and direct – you won't put this book down quickly.'

Sebastian Bates, founder of The Warrior Academy

'If, like me, you have a business and a brand, but no idea about branding, you need this book! Unless you have the skills and talents of both a marketing professional and a graphic designer, you are at risk of making some very expensive mistakes. Sapna's practical, down-to-earth advice will help you avoid that. Her book is full of great tips, activities and case studies that demystify the branding process and will help you develop your own thinking as well as find – and communicate better with – the right supplier. A great read!'

Antoinette Oglethorpe, leadership development coach, speaker, author

'Let's Get Visible! details Sapna's approach to branding with amazing clarity for any business owner, new or established. The VISION process helped me position my company to speak specifically to my target customer, and yet have enough breadth and longevity that I could expand into other markets with the same branding and messaging. Her VISION process is so effective, I've hired her as Brand Mentor for my company and she teaches what's in this book to my clients and customers!'

Alexander Seery, founder of Shifts to Success, author, coach

'Let's Get Visible! *is the book I wish I'd read when setting up my company. Practical, clear advice with useful case studies that bring the VISION process to life, I found myself reaching for a notepad before page 10!*

I found Sapna's emphasis on nurturing your brand a particularly useful concept, offering powerful questions to challenge any lurking brand complacency. She is clearly an expert and this book puts branding at the heart of commercial difference.'

Sara Milne Rowe, founder of Coaching Impact and author of *The Shed Method*

'Sapna is a branding genius and has an incredible ability to take thoughts, ideas and concepts from the minds of entrepreneurs and translate them into branding which looks amazing and which tells a story in itself. Throughout the book, Sapna outlines her method for building an incredible brand and provides insights on the importance of branding and why it's so essential for any business – new or established – to put in place branding which stands them out from the crowd.

Your business identity and branding says everything about who you are and if you want to stand out in a crowded market, then this book will help you plan and define what you need.'

James White, sales mentor and trainer, founder of Get Sales Fit

'The future of branding.'

Tim Pat, Magento Development

To my darling husband, Andy – my muse, inspiration and my absolute rock, without whom I could not have written this book.
To my boys, Luc and Leon – my driving forces and my personal 'why'.

Contents

Foreword

When I started my first business I needed a business card, a letterhead, a DL-width compliments slip, a one-page A5 and A4 information sheet and a brochure. I also needed a rate card, a price list and sign-up form, an invoice, and then a website and then something for a newspaper and magazine article... and something for a banner... and then something for a TV ad.

To me my brand was my logo. But here's what happened.

Firstly, I did these myself. And I didn't do these all at once. I created them in dribs and drabs over a couple of years. Then I went to a corporate identity workshop. They asked us to bring an example of *everything* that had our brand on it, so I grabbed everything with our logo on. Then they asked us to pin everything to a wall. I discovered I had 24 fonts, 13 colours and images that even to this day I have no idea why they were used. It looked a complete mess. When I was being influenced by corporate clients I went all serious and pretentious, but at other times my logo showed up as cursive script, futuristic, serifs, sans-serifs – you name it.

In fact, standing back it looked like my company had a complete personality bypass or an identity disorder. And even though I stripped everything back to two fonts and two colours, whilst it was a massive improvement the logo still didn't reflect who I was or wanted to be... and worse, it looked dated and tired and devoid of personality and spark.

The bottom line was that I had no idea what a brand was or just how important it was to the success of my business.

I have since worked with many branding experts and Sapna Pieroux is easily the person I would trust with my brand. Sapna had extensive industry experience managing world-famous brands before starting her own branding consultancy.

Very rarely do you find someone who gets brand to its fullest expression across a broad range of applications. And rarely do you meet a creative who can unpack how they are working the magic... who also sees the commercial imperative.

Sapna has created the VISION process so any business owner can understand what it takes to build a brand and clearly communicate the DNA of their brand to a designer. I have seen Sapna work with start-ups to design a branding solution from scratch, and I've also been blown away with how she has rebooted established brands.

I have looked at her client work and thought, 'Of course that's what was needed.' But in each case, the VISION process outlined in this book provided a clear structure for arriving at an elegant solution. And judging by testimonials and results, the approach delivers.

Let's Get Visible! walks you through Sapna's proven six-step VISION branding process. The results are that you will enter a creative branding process much better informed about the DNA of your brand and the ability to provide your creative with a much clearer brief.

I discovered the implications of getting it wrong... starting with opportunity cost. I am convinced that my early attempts at branding unsold potential good clients simply because I didn't understand the branding process.

If you are serious about attracting the right customers and financial success *Let's Get Visible!* is required reading.

Andrew Priestley, multi-award-winning business leadership coach,
Top 100 UK Entrepreneur Mentor 2017 and best-selling business author

Introduction

I've been drawing since I was two. Mainly elephants, I recall. Bizarrely, I always drew them upside-down, then I'd turn the page the right way up to add the details, flowers, trees and clouds.

Looking back, I wonder if this was the first sign that I like looking at things from both sides.

As a preschooler, I watched *Paint Along with Nancy* and meticulously followed Ms. Kominsky's televised oil-painting tutorials with my crayons. I drew obsessively and my drawings always seemed to make grown-ups happy, so I drew some more. I remember my indignation at the age of nine though when my schoolmates were convinced my parents had done my homework (my section of the Bayeux tapestry got an A++). It was all my own work!

How I used to draw elephants

After years of pestering, when I was eleven, my parents finally trusted me with oil paints and turps. I started painting landscapes and gifting them to family members and parent-friends. By the age of fifteen, I was being commissioned for oil portraits – my first entrepreneurial venture!

My first entrepreneurial venture?

Both my parents were NHS doctors and my dad, an eye surgeon, was keen that I should become an optician so he could refer all of his patients to me. When I announced I wanted to be a graphic designer, they were pretty worried. Neither of them understood that world. My dad thought I was 'wasting' my education. My form teacher said I was 'too bright'. Only my art teacher, Miss Hanlon, encouraged me to follow my passion.

Despite everyone's best efforts to set me on a different path, I eventually graduated from the University of Northumbria, one of the UK's leading design establishments (Sir Jonathan Ive of Apple fame is an alumnus). But even as a student, I realised that this amazing course, which had taught me everything about design, hadn't prepared me for the world of business. I took on a post-graduate diploma in marketing to understand more about business and how design would fit into the marketing mix.

My ambition was always to start a design agency with a business edge, but then I got a job offer from the marketing department at Metro Radio Group when they saw my final project. It wasn't in the plan, but it sounded exciting (and I figured I might get to meet Robbie Williams), so I accepted.

My twenty-five-year career spanned the design and media industries, marketing, advertising and creative sales. I've worked for Chrysalis, Emap Advertising, The Telegraph Media Group and O2 Media among others.

I've helped brands like Sony Ericsson, Mercedes Benz and Rimmel reach their target audiences with multimedia content-driven campaigns, winning a few awards along the way.

I swapped showbiz parties for birthday ones when I had my children, but after having my second baby, I was felled by post-natal depression. Suddenly feeling broken, fragile and incapable, I knew that going back to my previous fast-paced, high-pressure, hard-partying career and lifestyle was unthinkable. Just getting showered and out of the house before 11am felt like a huge achievement.

I took three years out to focus on my babies and heal myself with cognitive behavioural therapy (CBT) and running. I completed a half-marathon for Cancer Research in memory of my best friend, Lizzy, project-managed my own loft extension, volunteered for a local parenting group, fought off septicaemia (eight days in intensive care, amazing staff, wonderful friends and one stubborn me, refusing to die). I also completed a second degree in interior design with distinction and a plan to build a new home-based career around my little family.

Meanwhile, a few friends and my husband Andy had started their own businesses and asked me to help with their logos, brochures and websites. Andy's brochure got held up at a large entrepreneurial event by author and award-winning business coach Andrew Priestley, no less, who told everyone that this was 'the gold standard'.

Andy came home that evening to find me with a baby in my arms and a toddler at my legs, and handed me a fistful of business cards. Seven people who had never met me wanted to work with me. I realised my new business venture had been staring me in the face all along.

InnerVisions ID officially launched in 2016. I combined my design know-how with my commercial experience in marketing, sales and advertising to create my unique six-step VISION process (Visualise, Inner Brand, Stand Out, Image, Output, Nurture) which results in what I call 'branding that means business'.

The brochure that started it all...

With clients in the UK, Europe, America and Australia, InnerVisions ID now provides international brand expertise for ambitious entrepreneurs across the world who want to make a difference.

Since the business launched, I've been published three times as a co-author, have written for *The Huffington Post* and have won a Women In Business Rising Star Award, but I am most proud to be the brand mentor for a national programme called *Shifts to Success*, helping police officers and members of the NHS transition into a life of entrepreneurship.

This book is for you if you are an ambitious entrepreneur, business owner or brand manager. Your business may be new or it may have been going several years. You may have no branding, you may have some. You may feel the branding you got was never quite right, or you've outgrown it and it doesn't represent your company now, nor how you want to be perceived in the future. You may want to launch with power or move your business to the next level. You may want to grow your business so you can help more people, or expand into new services, appeal to a new demographic or territories, or get your business ready for investment. If you found yourself nodding along to any of the above, you're in the right place.

There is an overwhelming amount of content – posts, downloads, quizzes, blogs, videos, photos and more – being produced every day by people, including your competitors, all vying for your customers' time and money. It's more difficult than ever to gain cut-through. If your competitors are making more of an impact than you and you can't get a customer's attention in the first few seconds, then it's easy to become lost in the information tsunami, invisible to your prospects.

You need to stand out and differentiate yourself from the crowd.

Let's Get Visible! will change the way you look at branding and help you harness its true power to transform your business.

Over my career, I've had the unusual experience of working as both the designer and the client where I've had to brief designers. I've experienced the challenges and the frustrations on both sides. My unique background meant that when I started my company, I approached things differently. I would naturally look at the business issues first, and then use design strategically as a tool to help solve them.

I also really enjoyed teaching my clients about branding and helping them to create a brand that really supported their business aspirations. They would tell me that what I did was 'so much more than design'; that I brought amazing clarity to them and their business; that they loved the collaborative way I worked; that they'd never worked in this way before, feeling so involved and invested in the final design solutions.

As a fellow entrepreneur, I understood that we generally like being in control of our destiny, so it was only natural to me that my clients would want some input into their branding. I designed my enjoyable and easy VISION process to be a collaborative process between client and designer.

That's why *Let's Get Visible!* is written for you, the business owner, so you can understand branding, align it to your business goals and use it to help grow your business.

This book will *not* teach you how to design and it's not going to put any designers out of work – in fact, I recommend that you use a professional every time. I'll even give you tips on finding one. The VISION process will help you develop and grow your brand from the fundamentals up. You will learn about your hidden brand aspirations, find your brand voice and understand your industry branding clichés – and how to avoid them. VISION will help you build a brand that you and your customers will love.

Understanding the power of branding will give you remarkable brand clarity, help you stand out in your industry and supercharge your business growth.

Before we get started, I would like to share a lovely observation a friend made on reading this introduction:

> *'Isn't it funny that your dad was an eye surgeon helping others to see and now you're using your VISION process to make others more visible?'*

Strange how life turns out, eh?

This book is split into three parts.

In Part 1, we look at the fascinating history and rise of the brand. We define the difference between brand, branding and personal branding. We look at the three main problems entrepreneurs typically experience before they get branded. Finally, my DoSaySee model neatly illustrates the big mistake most entrepreneurs make when it comes to their branding, and what you really need to build your brand.

Part 2 takes you through my six-step VISION process, which is when the magic happens.

Then in Part 3, I will help you find a designer, understand their world, learn about various production techniques and speak their lingo.

To get the most out of this book, I suggest you read the whole thing through on your own first, then:

- Complete the branding assessment if you have an existing company and are rebranding (skip this step if you are a start-up with no branding)

- Go through 'Visualise' and 'Inner Brand', either on your own or with other major stakeholders in the business

- At the 'Stand Out' stage, things start to get visual, so you can do this alone or choose to involve your designer

- For 'Image', 'Output' and 'Nurture', you will need to partner up with a professional designer

You'll find it useful to create a digital mood board as we will use this for a lot of the exercises in the book. Use Pinterest, PowerPoint or Keynotes – anywhere you can place inspirational images and track your brand development throughout the VISION process, adding, reordering or deleting as you go.

We like Pinterest as our clients can collaborate and annotate pins with us in real time (you can make shared boards 'secret' if confidentiality is an issue too). Your digital mood board will develop your visual literacy and understanding of brands, especially what you like and don't like. Use it to brief your designer, photographer, web developer – any creative who is helping you develop your brand. Your communication will become much more visual as a result, rather than just relying on the written or spoken word, and will bring a lot more clarity to the whole process for everyone,

Part 1
Understanding
Branding

The Rise Of The Brand

'If this business were to be split up, I would be glad to take the brands, trademarks and goodwill and you could have all the bricks and mortar – and I would fare better than you.'

John Stuart, former chairman of Quaker Oats

At least since fire was invented, humankind has used branding as a mark of ownership or identification. As we began to domesticate animals, a hot iron 'brand' was used to burn a distinctive shape, symbol or mark into their skin to signify them as belonging to a certain family or tribe. In Ancient Rome, and even in colonial times, slave owners did the same to mark their human 'property'. In the 1500s, branding the face or hands was used to permanently identify criminals in society, so it became a 'mark of disgrace or stigma'.[1] The accused would have to hold their hands up in court to show if they'd ever been convicted before (I wonder if this is why people still have to put their hand up when they swear their oath on the Bible?).

Thankfully, this barbaric practice was outlawed in England by the 1800s, we now live in more enlightened times, slavery has been abolished, branding has evolved and I'm not in the business of burning cows or criminals for a living.

Since the era of manufacturing and transportation, which made nationwide distribution possible, the range of products and services available to consumers has no longer been based on locality. The things people bought didn't have

---

1   www.dictionary.com

to be sold by their local butcher, baker or candlestick maker – now they could buy a loaf of, say, Hovis bread or a bar of Pear's soap anywhere in the land.

Brands and branding really took off in the 1950s when television became popular and visual messaging became possible nationwide. This was the *Mad Men* era, advertising and marketing's glamorous and golden heyday. Brand domination was achieved 'top down' for national advertisers with big budgets via mainstream broadcast media – TV, radio, press and posters – and messages and images were carefully crafted by the manufacturers and their ad agencies. For example, soap powder manufacturers funded TV drama series that appealed to housewives (ever wondered where the term 'soap opera' came from?).

Meanwhile, medical research was beginning to find evidence that smoking may be bad for you, so the government started banning images of doctors sparking up and any health claims related to smoking on advertising. The brand promise *'They're toasted to taste better'* (its conception dramatised and immortalised by Don Draper in the first ever episode of *Mad Men*) not only complied with the new messaging guidelines but cleverly played to Lucky Strike cigarette brand's unique selling point. Using celebrities also gave the brand more standout and caché than their competitors.

Fast forward to the twenty-first century and the worldwide web. The proliferation of digital media in the early 2000s meant the bottom fell out of the advertising industry. Traditional platforms have struggled ever since and many print titles have folded in the last twenty years. Diminishing ad budgets are being spread over an increasing number of channels, while bigger brands are competing with newer, smaller upstarts and have struggled to reach the brand domination they once had.

Lucky Strike ad, 1950s, featuring golf champion Sam Snead

For smaller businesses, start-ups and entrepreneurs, though, the digital boom meant cheaper technology and distribution, so it became easier than ever to reach and serve an international customer base. Teenagers are now running global retail businesses from their bedrooms via Instagram. Virtual assistants in the Philippines are looking after business owners worldwide over cloud-based systems. My own agency, based in west London, works with clients across several continents. Savvy marketers are taking matters into their own hands, building communities of brand fans on social media, engaging with 'influencers' and producing entertaining or powerful video content which goes viral for a fraction of the cost of traditional media.

Information about a company's brand is now no longer broadcast from the top down, but rather generated by customers from the ground up.

What exactly is a brand?

Many entrepreneurs think their logo is their brand or branding, and they use those words interchangeably. A logo is *not* your brand. Nobody ever felt loyal or passionate about a company because of its logo.

Think of your favourite brands: the ones you wear, use or eat regularly; a place you shop; a favourite media channel; a trusted car manufacturer... You may feel loyal to them, passionate about them. You may tell all your family and friends about them. You may feel part of a group, an in-crowd or tribe. Your chosen brands say something about you and the life you lead.

Far from just being a logo, a brand is often defined as the sum of everything your company does as perceived by others

It's every touchpoint your customers or potential customers experience – from first contact to leaving a review. Your brand is your company's image, people, products or services, messaging, values, the environment in which you operate and how all of that makes your customers, staff and suppliers *feel*. I would add that your brand is now how it is communicated by these people. Or as Jeff Bezos, founder of Amazon, famously put it in his 2012 TED Talk:

> *'Your brand is what other people say about you when you're not in the room.'*

Brand is a snowballing of all those experiences, perceptions, feelings and thoughts. The more momentum you generate, the bigger that snowball gets. Positive experiences build brand fans, advocates, five-star reviews, partnerships, referrals, reputation, repeat business and a loyalty that can carry a company through the rough times. On the flip side, bad customer reviews can destroy your brand far faster than you built it.

Brands live or die by information so easily relayed peer-to-peer. This means that, rather worryingly for any entrepreneur, your brand is sometimes out of your control.

What is personal branding?

A lot of my clients confuse personal branding (which my company doesn't do) with branding (which we do) – especially those whose company name is their own name. Both branding and personal branding help build your business, but they are very different creatures.

When you start your business, you may just get by on the strength of your reputation and personality alone, especially if you've had an illustrious career, are well-connected and well-liked in your industry. But if you're entering a new market, hiring more staff or opening new offices, as you scale, you simply can't be everywhere. Even when your part-time virtual assistant sends your client an email, your company brand is now bigger than you.

Your personal and business brands should ideally be treated as two separate but complementary entities (think Stella McCartney the person and Stella McCartney the fashion label). Your personal brand centres around you as an individual, the face of your company. This includes:

- How you show up in real life and online
- Your professional character and personality, public opinions, views and thoughts
- Your image: body language, wardrobe, grooming, voice
- Your reputation and how you manage it, especially in times of crisis

There are image consultants, stylists, presentation and voice coaches, to help, even companies that 'clean up' your online personal brand history if absolutely necessary.

Elon Musk, Richard Branson, Sheryl Sandberg and Oprah Winfrey all have powerful personal brands. Of course, each is so closely linked to their company brand that any negative press around them or their companies can affect the perception of both. Michelle Obama has a great personal brand. Loved for her authentic family values, views and achievements, she is intelligent and honest, not afraid to address serious issues, yet she's also witty, funny and self-deprecating. (Watch her appearance on James Corden's *Carpool Karaoke* to see what I mean.[2])

---

2   www.youtube.com/watch?v=In3wAdRAim4

Michelle uses personal branding cleverly to communicate her status. When she was the President's wife, Michelle patriotically championed US designers with chic, demure tailored dresses befitting of her role, but on the last night of her book tour in 2018, she rocked up wearing $4,000 thigh-high Balenciaga silver-sequinned boots and a silky yellow dress, split daringly to the thigh. That one outfit told us in no uncertain terms that her life had changed and she was definitely enjoying the freedom of not being First Lady.

First impressions count

As with your branding, paying attention to details with your personal branding will make a great first impression and either help you win business, or cost you more than you know. Looking, sounding and acting the part will allow your amazing knowledge and personality to shine through without your audience being distracted by an ill-fitting outfit, verbal or physical tics, or the spinach on your teeth.

As first impressions land in the first few seconds, if you are looking to take your business up a level, consider re-evaluating your personal brand image too, as I did when I started to get more speaking roles. I'd been filmed at one of my first events wearing a loose-fitting COS black dress. I thought I looked smart, professional and designer-chic (COS is popular with designers), but on screen, I looked shapeless. My dress blended into the dark-clad crowd and all anyone could see was a 'floating head'!

My image consultant, the amazing Jo Baldwin Trott, confirmed that fashionista-favourite black is a colour 'to hide in'. After a colour consultation (I cannot recommend this enough), she took me shopping. In came bright red, fuchsia pink, cobalt blue and emerald green in sharper cuts. My new speaker wardrobe helped me create more impact on stage.

I still wear black for meetings. It's thankfully in my colour palette (I'm a 'Cool Winter') and ties in with my personal brand as a designer. It's also one of my company brand colours so I'll often pair it with a pop of red, my other brand colour. Wearing your company colours to meetings or events is a great way to look 'on brand' and imprint your image in people's minds.

If you really want to make an impression with a client, especially if you are meeting them for the first time, you might even wear one of *their* brand colours. You can do this subtly with an accessory or even a note-book. They will feel more connected to you in those vital first few seconds and probably won't even realise why.

Wearing my client Alex's brand colours

If you feel you need a personal image overhaul, you can hire an image consultant or personal brand specialist like I did. Alternatively, department stores offer free personal styling sessions, so take advantage and book yourself in. Brief them and they will go off to find what you need whilst you relax in a private room. A personal rebrand will help you feel more confident, look better and make fewer mistakes, just like a company rebrand.

Branding for business

Have you ever been put off dealing with a business when you see an awful business card? A clunky website? A scruffy salesperson? Typos? If a business doesn't look the part, it won't fill you with confidence. Within just six seconds, you'll have made up your mind – to look elsewhere.

If your brand is the sum of your customer experiences, branding makes your brand promise 'real', tangible and recognisable.

Your branding is about how your company looks, feels and communicates your brand promise to the world. Discovering your brand values, personality and voice, and then conveying them consistently through messaging and visuals is what will help create the emotional connection. When people feel connected and aligned to your brand, they become loyal fans, repeat customers and passionate advocates for your company.

Branding is the first touch-point your audience will have with your brand; it's how your brand makes that great first impression. In the same way that you'd pay attention to your appearance for an important meeting, branding is your business dressing for success. This is important for you as an entrepreneur as you (likely) don't have the power of a big or well-known brand behind you.

The VISION process brings your and your customer's visions together to establish that emotional connection. In Part 2 of this book, you will learn how to choose branding elements to affect your audience on a conscious, subconscious and psychological level. Sounds complex, but my simple six-step VISION process will guide you through it all. Oh, and unlike your brand, your branding is completely within your control.

As Steve Forbes said:

> *'Your brand is the single most important investment you can make in your business.'*

Great branding helps your brand stand out and gain visibility in your industry. Getting noticed is the vital first step to anyone taking action.

In an increasingly cluttered visual landscape, your branding, used consistently, will help your customers clearly and easily recognise your content among the noise. If your business shows up looking professional and polished, it inspires more confidence and trust in your customers. They will be much more likely to believe that you will make an effort with their custom too. Branding can help you communicate your vision and values more clearly and connect with potential clients on a deeper emotional or psychological level. When they understand what makes you different and better, customers will feel more engaged and be less likely to shop around as their decision is no longer just price-led.

According to *Circle Research,* 77% of B2B marketing leaders say branding is critical to business growth – and branding can actually *make* you money. The average revenue increase attributed to always presenting a brand consistently is 23%.[3] It makes sense that in a world full of uncertainty, a company that demonstrates consistency is going to make customers feel that its standards and service will be similarly reliable. And if you are thinking of your exit strategy, branding will boost the value of your business to investors, so it's definitely an asset and investment.

---

3   Source: *Lucidpress*

In addition to all these well-documented business benefits of branding, I've also seen first-hand that it can make entrepreneurs' ambitions come alive. This is no insignificant task. One of my clients says that having an idea for a business is like being pregnant. The idea may be there, but no one knows what it will look like. Branding, he says, is like the baby being born: it is now real and visible to the world.

Just like the best makeovers, I marvel at the personal transformation I see after I've worked with entrepreneurs. Their increased confidence in and energy for their business is almost magical.

When your branding is on point, you're likely to be amazed how much more confident you will feel. You will look more established, professional and successful. Branding is not about faking it till you make it (you do need a quality product or service to back it up), but about having everything aligned to communicate the quality of what you do. This helps you and your team to be proud of your company image and have the confidence to go for the business you want. I've had clients who were previously too embarrassed to hand out their business cards (which is a sure-fire way to make sure people *don't* call you).

Beautiful branding can even attract your ideal clients at first sight. Rebecca Godfrey of Etheo Ltd says that time and time again, people comment favourably on her branding, one client even going so far as to say that when he saw her branding, he knew immediately that he wanted to work with her.

Another client, Marie-Clare, finally found the courage to quit her day job and follow her passion to start her own catering business once she got her branding in place (she'd been doing catering as a paid hobby in the evenings and at weekends until then).

Etheo branding elements .
Top, L-R: logo, method model, business cards, LinkedIn profile

Alexander Seery, founder of Shifts to Success, attracted investment from a global venture capitalist within months of starting his company. Whilst he clearly had a great business idea, he knows that his branding helped him launch with confidence, impact and helped him look the part.

These examples prove that whatever your ambitions are, branding can help you achieve them, and I'm not exaggerating when I say it can literally change your life.

The three main problems

Having worked almost exclusively with entrepreneurs for the last few years, I have identified the three main problems that they typically experience:

- Resource
- Clarity
- Visibility

The Resource problem

'I can't afford to brand.'

Money, people and time are resources that are in short supply for many entrepreneurs, especially when they are starting out. They may be trying to save money, or scared to delegate or hand control over to someone else, so they end up running around like a headless chicken, doing lots of things not very well. Branding gets shoved further down the priority list as a 'nice to have' rather than an essential part of their business arsenal. They decide they will sort out their branding properly 'when they can afford it' or 'when they get enough clients'. They may even feel it a bit frivolous to spend money on 'appearances'.

With no tangible brand differentiation, you can fall into a vicious spiral of price-led conversations, attracting clients who will haggle, want the moon on a stick for free, will be a pain-in-the-bum. They won't thank you; instead, they'll zap what's left of your time and energy and you'll make less money.

You need *something*, though, so you may do it yourself, ask 'a mate with a Mac' or try cheap design sites, but a lack of knowledge, technology and/or skills means these routes take ages and still end up not looking 'right'. Worse still, potential clients may be put off working with you because of it, judging this lack of care for your own company as an indication that your standards may not be so high for them either. There's a dentist a two-minute walk from where I live, yet I have rejected going to them based solely on appearances: the signage outside is terrible – scruffy and dated – so I imagine the interior, equipment and the dentist's aesthetics will be similarly lacking.

You deserve more. Investment in your branding attracts the right clients more easily and will give you a return on investment (ROI) in ways you can't yet foresee or necessarily predict. It will open doors and opportunities that may have otherwise been closed. It will give you more confidence and people will take you more seriously. One of my clients raised the price for a product from £1,600 to £2,600 after their rebrand. Nothing else had changed, but they felt more confident to ask for more once they looked more premium. Another client sold her highest-value package (£5,000) on her first ever sale in her new business. Her own immaculate image plus her luxurious-looking, elegant branding quietly communicated the professionalism and quality

Before

After

of her premium offering and her attention to detail, leaving her clients confident she could do a quality job for them too.

A client had her IT developers create a logo for a new piece of software she was going to sell into schools. She needed a new brochure, but I knew it was going to be impossible to create a great design with the logo she had, so I gently told her, 'I think you deserve better.'

If you were a headteacher, which company would you trust to deliver on their promise to protect your pupils' welfare?

Not realising or believing in the value of good design is endemic in our society. So many of my clients are almost embarrassed to admit they don't know much about branding. They know what they like when they see it, but they usually don't know how to articulate what they want, or if a design looks 'wrong', they don't know what will make it look right.

In her book *Drawing on the Right Side of the Brain*, Betty Edwards observes that most people's art education stalls at around the age of eight. Ask most adults to draw a house, they'll likely do it the same way they did as a child: a rectangle with a triangle on top for a roof and more rectangles for windows, a door and perhaps a chimney (if they're feeling flash).

If this describes you, it's not your fault. The arts have never been properly funded (in the UK at least), so teaching children even an *appreciation* of art and design within our already-squeezed education system is simply not a priority.

This makes me so sad as an arts-enriched education is proven to boost happiness, decision-making, analytical and creative thinking, and enhance overall behaviour and results.[4]

Helen Russell in her book *The Year of Living Danishly* identifies an appreciation of the arts as one of the factors that makes Denmark consistently rated the happiest country in the world.

Indeed, my bigger hope for this book is that once you've invested in your branding and seen the difference it makes to yourself, your business and your customers, you will start seeing the world around you differently too.

Still think you can't afford to brand?

The Clarity problem

'I have no idea about branding.'

You may not know where to start, lack confidence, clarity, knowledge, language, skills or time, or just want someone to take it all away and do it for you. You may feel overwhelmed and lack focus. You may not understand what goes into branding; what you want or need; what to ask for. You may have already wasted money and time on things which didn't work. You may have been 'burnt' by bad experiences or designers, found the design process vague and stressful, or been intimidated or confused by 'creative types' and their jargon. You may keep trying different things but nothing 'sticks', resulting in muddled 'throw everything at it' thinking.

---

[4]   www.kqed.org/mindshift/50874/what-happens-to-student-behavior-when-schools-prioritize-art

Constant trial and error leads to a messy, inconsistent look and incoherent brand communications, and a lack of clarity only confuses your potential customers. I've had clients who admitted they'd previously paid for design they didn't really like. Maybe they had no clarity on what they needed or didn't know how to articulate what they wanted. It may sound strange, but design that doesn't make you feel amazing when you look at it will reflect on you and your business, weighing you down silently every day. By contrast, my clients report renewed clarity, focus and direction once they are branded properly. They feel more aligned, energised and ready to move forward. Some have even likened it to therapy for the difference it makes to their very being.

One client confessed that she 'felt a big shift and emotional change' when she rebranded with us. 'Powerful stuff,' she reflected. Her increased confidence and business growth gave her the impetus to change other areas of her life too. She even joined a local band as lead vocalist – she used to sing when she was younger but hadn't felt the drive to do so in years until the rebrand.

For your clients, brand clarity and consistency build recognition, understanding, familiarity and trust as your company looks established, professional and sure of itself. It will attract clients because when you put clarity out there, people will start seeking it from you.

A lack of clarity can exist in the designer/client relationship, too. Designers don't generally understand businesspeople and businesspeople don't generally understand designers. On my graphic design degree, we were not prepared for the world of business, and when I studied marketing, design wasn't really addressed at all. It was mentioned only as part of the marketing mix. Unsurprisingly, designers and marketers end up speaking in tongues to each other. This lack of a common language often leads to a disconnect, a communications gap, frustration and disappointing results.

When I worked as a designer at agencies, non-designers (clients, account handlers) were called the 'suits' and seen as 'the other'. Unintelligible, or at best vague briefs were to be expected, and a client's feedback or requests were often seen as compromising the creative output. When I was client-side, I found it just as frustrating when designers didn't show an interest in my business objectives, went off on creative tangents that were inappropriate or threw so many ideas at me, they were clearly just hoping something would stick.

I realised that designers and businesspeople can approach the same brief with radically differing objectives, too. Designers generally love to create things of beauty, get praised for their work, perhaps even win awards. A lot of designers are quite introverted and won't question your brief, assuming you know what you need. They are rarely business strategists, marketers, copywriters and editors, so they will tend to unquestioningly take what they've been given and try to make it look good.

Businesspeople tend to want to get things done as quickly and/or cheaply as they can. They put a lot of faith in their designer, give them all the control as they don't know what they are doing, but often end up frustrated or with an unexpected result if the communication isn't clear or the designer misunderstands what they thought was a clear brief. If you've ever watched BBC's *The Apprentice*, you'll realise that never in the show's history has any businessperson seemingly understood what 'luxury packaging' should look like!

A common design journey goes like this: client gives designer a brief. Designer takes brief and goes off to create. Designer is not sure exactly what the client wants, so they present a range of options. Client is confused by the choice, or nothing hits the spot. Designer can't really help as they are confused too. No one admits to being confused. Client is not sure what they want, but this isn't what they had in mind. A lot of to-ing and fro-ing and revisions ensue. Client and designer slowly, silently lose their minds, before they get to the final signed-off artwork.

In a *Design Week* article *'How To Impress When Presenting Work To Clients'*, John Scarrott warned designers presenting their work that:

> *'... This is their first sight of your work. Bringing [the client] up to speed on what you've developed will take more than "voila", followed by a flourish. And that's why you need to spend more time thinking and preparing how you will get your client to love your work as much as you do, and how to manage the situation and yourself if they don't.'*

I commented on his article, John shared my thoughts and we ended up having a great conversation in real life. My view is that any design solution shouldn't need lots of explaining and persuasion. The client's target audience won't have the benefit of the designer's wisdom, so the work needs to speak for itself. Also, if designers involve their clients throughout the process, they won't need to 'sell in' their design work.

Graphic design used to be known as 'commercial art', and I believe that it should actually be a perfect blend of both business and creativity. The VISION process takes both parties on a collaborative journey. When client and designer work more closely together, understanding and communication are vastly improved. This level of clarity means that typically, our clients sign off their creative within the first round of designs.

What else could you achieve with all that increased clarity around your business?

The Visibility problem

How do we stand out from the competition?'

Whilst the technological revolution and the internet have created a huge opportunity for entrepreneurs, they have also created a huge challenge. An overwhelming amount of content is being published every day on a global scale. There are 500 hours of video uploaded per minute and 1 billion hours are watched every day on YouTube alone.[5] Then there's Instagram, Facebook, LinkedIn, Twitter, Snapchat, Vimeo, newspapers, posters, flyers, magazines, brochures, radio, TV, cinema, online. . .

A search on Google in September 2019 showed:

- There are more than 575 million registered users on LinkedIn[6]

- 500 million tweets are posted daily[7]

- More than 350 million photos are uploaded to Facebook every day[8]

- Users 'like' 4.2 billion posts per day on Instagram[9]

- 1.6 billion websites with 500 million blogs on the internet[10]

- There are 23 million YouTube channels and 700,000 active podcasts on iTunes[11]

---

5   www.statista.com/statistics/259477/hours-of-video-uploaded-to-youtube-every-minute/, May 2019
6   www.kinsta.com/blog/linkedin-statistics
7   www.internetlivestats.com/twitter-statistics
8   www.brandwatch.com/blog/facebook-statistics
9   www.blog.hootsuite.com/instagram-statistics
10 www.hostingtribunal.com/blog/how-many-blogs
11 www.tubics.com/blog/number-of-youtube-channels, www.musicoomph.com/podcast-statistics

Everyone who is online – not just your direct competitors – is distracting your customers and vying for their time and money. How on earth do you get noticed when a Google search for 'business coaches', for example, brings up (at time of writing) about 232,000,000 results in 0.68 seconds (up from 189 million when I started writing this book)?

The rate of new businesses launching is rising every year: a massive 99.9% of the 5.7 million businesses in the UK are classed as small or medium-sized enterprises (SMEs) with fewer than 250 employees.[12] Search engine optimisation (SEO) and content help, of course, but if your competitors are doing the same, the need to stand out and look better than them is essential to scaling your business.

As design guru Raymond Loewy said:

> 'Between two products equal in price, function and quality, the one with the most attractive exterior will win.'

Not being visible enough means that you are losing business right now to your better-looking competitors. Not better, just better-looking. How shallow and soul-destroying is that? For all the effort you're making, if you're not being noticed by your audience, you may as well be invisible.

We are simply visual creatures. We seek visual clues first to understand the world, what's good for us and what's not.

Human female fertility is indicated by a higher hip to waist ratio. This is why the hourglass shape is seen as 'sexy' and middle-aged spread isn't. We look at the colour of a banana to gauge its ripeness or we see mould on our bread

---

12   www.merchantsavvy.co.uk/uk-sme-data-stats-charts

and decide it's not good to eat. Symmetrical facial features and bodies are deemed more attractive because they indicate a healthier gene pool and a disease-free upbringing.

Things that look 'good' are generally better for us and our survival. This is why we decide whether we want to do business with someone within seven seconds of meeting them – based on little other than visual cues.[13]

Diminishing attention spans have now given rise to short-form advertising on social media where brands have to make an impact in six seconds or fewer – and they have to look good to do that. A friend in property tells me that home-seekers take an average of 2.5 seconds before they reject a property. This is the biggest spend they will make in their lives, so how quickly might they reject a business based on appearance alone?

Ever felt love at first sight? You feel great when you're with that loved one, perhaps look cooler when you're with them, spend more money on them. You talk about them all the time and share your happiness on social media. Your friends may even ask how you found them, especially if they hope to duplicate your success.

I'm talking about brands, of course. The kind of love that makes us do really crazy things. It's why Chanel can sell a pair of skis for thousands. The same rules apply to your business. When your branding is working for you, customers will be attracted to and feel instantly connected with your brand. But just as in love, being noticed is the first step in building a relationship, so if you're not catching and keeping people's attention because you aren't visible enough, you're missing out.

---

13   *Forbes*, Seven Seconds to make a First Impression, Carol Kinsey Goman PhD, Feb 13 2011, www.forbes.com/sites/carolkinseygoman/2011/02/13/seven-seconds-to-make-a-first-impression

Your Brand Foundations

'The best and most successful brands are completely coherent. Every aspect of what they are and what they do reinforces everything else.'

Wally Olins, design legend

In my time working with entrepreneurs, I have identified a repeating pattern in how they built their businesses and seen the big mistake that so many of them made. They simply weren't aligning their branding with their business goals. This was not helping them get to where they wanted to be – and in some cases, it was even holding them back.

I developed my DoSaySee model to help entrepreneurs understand the three important pillars of building a successful brand:

1. What you *Do*

2. What you *Say*

3. What people *See*

Do: when you start a business, you first focus on what you *Do*. It's ultimately how you will make a difference and make a living, so it is vital to get this right. What you Do is the problem you are solving; the products or services that you sell. What makes you different from your competition? What's your customer experience? Do will also include your business plan, target market, vision and values, delivery, technology and processes, premises and staff.

The DoSaySee Model

Say: next, you focus on how to tell the world what you're doing. This encompasses the written or spoken word. You may read business books, invest in coaches or copywriters, check out your competition or go networking to hone your message. Say includes everything from your business name and strapline to your pitch and how you speak about your business. It's the copy on your website, brochure, social media posts, in your blogs, articles, white papers and book. Your Say will also form a part of your branding in your brand voice.

See: Your See is the first impression people will get of your brand. This includes your logo, but see incorporates *everything* visible about your company: your colours, typography, imagery, website, business cards and brochures, images, even the paper stock you choose. Your See is also how you present yourself and the environment you conduct your business in. Do you meet clients in Starbucks or a nice hotel? Is your office smart and professional or scruffy and messy?

Like a three-legged stool, your DoSaySee elements need to balance, align with and support one another to build a strong brand that resonates with your target market. Take any one leg away and the stool topples over. The red areas in the diagram highlight the 'danger zones' when any one of these elements is missing or out of sync.

An *insincere* business is when a company looks the part and promises you the world but then fails to deliver (no Do). A business that consistently or knowingly disappoints its customers is ultimately not honest or sustainable. One of the craziest examples of this was Fyre, the biggest 'luxury music festival' that never happened. Billy McFarland defrauded investors and festival goers of over $27million using glamorous Instagram pictures of supermodels, yachts and tales of luxe accommodation. He was later jailed for six years.

An incoherent business (no Say) is one that has a great offering and image to match, but what it says doesn't quite match up, whether written or spoken. If the copy on a website doesn't make sense or you can't easily find the information you need, you'll look elsewhere. Another common example of this is when you go on a website and the homepage has typos on it. I've rejected hiring designers in the past if their websites say they design 'stationary'.

An invisible business (no See) exists when, despite it having a great product or service and a clear message, it is let down by its branding. Lack of a polished image will lose a company business to a more attractive-looking competitor. This can happen when prospects are handed a tacky-looking business card or a website looks dated and loads slowly. These things almost imperceptibly, even subconsciously, cast doubt on the quality of the product or service.

The big mistake I see entrepreneurs make is that their See is so often not aligned with or given the same attention and importance as their Do and Say. It's not prioritised, not properly considered, a do it yourself (DIY) job or done on the cheap and treated like an afterthought. But if you align your See to support and strengthen your Do and Say, you will find amazing brand clarity and business growth, and your business will truly stand out.

In *How To Make People Like You In 90 Seconds Or Less*, Nicholas Boothman observes that 'if you want others to believe that you can be trusted you must be congruent'.

You know what it's like when someone tells you they're fine, yet their voice is flat, their arms are crossed and they can't look you in the eye? Inconsistency and incongruity bother people.

Boothman also talked about Albert Mehrabian who famously discovered that:

- 7% of people's understanding comes from the words you say (i.e. copy)

- 38% of understanding comes from the *way* you say it(i.e. brand voice or tone)

- 55% of understanding comes from your facial expressions and body language (i.e. the visuals)

I was delighted to realise that my DoSaySee model mirrors human behaviour. As a customer, you are attracted to a business first by what you see, just like you are with people. It's only once you like the look of someone that you may decide to speak to them... and only once you speak to them will you find out what they do. This is how any relationship is built – including those with your customers:

1. Do I like the look of this company?

2. Does it speak to and/or understand me?

3. What does the company do?

See, Say and Do, in that order. See?

DoSaySee exercise

Take a piece of paper or open up a blank document on your laptop and create three columns: Do, Say and See. List all the elements you will need to build your brand under each.

Do: the functional and vital elements of your business:

- What you actually do, i.e. the products and services you sell

- The equipment, processes, systems and software you need

- The people you need to help you fulfil your business (suppliers, partners, staff)

- How you will sell your product (online, offline, one-to-one, one-to-many)

- Delivery (online, transport, packaging, couriers)

Do may also include your bigger purpose, your 'why'.

Say: the written and spoken word, how your offering is communicated. This includes:

- Company name

- Strapline (positioning statement)

- Vision or mission statement

- Elevator, social and formal pitch

- Social media

- Website copy

- Brochure/flyer copy

- Blogs

- Book

- Talks

- What others say (reviews, reputation)

- Your brand voice

See: everything visual. This may include your:

- Logo

- Strapline (this is Say, but it is often a part of a logo too)

- Business cards, brochure/flyer designs

- Website design

- Social media imagery and posts

- Merchandise

- Branding scheme (colours, typefaces, imagery, etc)

- Image: yours and your staff's (personal branding, dress code)

- Business environment (professional, aspirational)

Under each heading, list what you have in place already and what you need. You can use this as a basic tick-list for all your business to-dos, but this exercise clearly demonstrates that you can't just fill two columns and leave the third one empty. The content of each column has got to align with and support the others to create your authentic brand.

Branding assessment

If you have an existing company, you will probably already possess an element of brand recognition, no matter how good – or bad – your current branding is.

If, like me, you love a percentage score, you might at this stage also wish to take our Brand Assets Health Check at www.InnerVisions-ID.com/quiz/

If you have more time, the fuller branding assessment that I will outline below is an additional pre-step, designed to take stock of where you are right now before we start the full VISION process. It's a litmus test to see what can stay, what needs to change and what needs to be banished from your company forthwith! Time to make like Japanese tidy-upper extraordinaire Marie Kondo and be sure that every aspect of your branding 'sparks joy'.

Use your See list and collate every branded aspect of your company, printed and digital. If you can, have examples or visuals of everything in front of you:

- Printed: business cards, brochures, workbooks, folders, flyers, books, stationery

- Functional: on/offline order forms, invoices, statements, etc

- Online: website, splash pages, sign-up and appointment booking forms, webinars, scorecards, social media pages and posts

- 3D/other: event signage, branded merchandise, packaging

Look at them with a critical eye; think as a potential customer. Do the exercise with someone trusted who has a good eye and will be honest with you (not family members or friends who may just tell you what you want to hear. Clients or peers with great branding will be a good shout).

- What would you say about the overall branding scheme?

- Does it all 'go' together or not?

- How does it make you *feel*?

- What about each brand element? Name? Logo? Strapline? Imagery? Type? Colours? Layouts?

- Are there any brand elements or assets that are missing?

- Do you need to start everything from scratch or is it a case of evolution rather than revolution?

I then categorise each branding element with a 'traffic light' system. It's *highly* technical; I just colour them green, orange or red:

- **Green**: what you like about your current branding and want to keep. Include what works and why.

- **Orange**: what you have already that needs to be tweaked, improved or simplified. Include elements that could be upcycled, e.g. photography from a previous shoot that could have a filter added to give it new life.

- **Red**: what doesn't work and either needs to go or be completely redesigned. Include what is missing and needs creating from scratch.

Don't think about *how* to change things at this stage, because the VISION process will give you that creative direction. Just keep your branding assessment in mind as you go through the book.

I understand that if you've had the same branding for a while, you may be nervous of change for fear of losing the brand equity and recognition you already have. Keep an open mind, though. What you love and want to keep, as familiar and comfortable as an old pair of slippers, may not be serving you best for now or for the future, so may also benefit from a nip and tuck. This is why new eyes can be helpful.

At the start of a rebrand project for Centenary Lounge, a 1930s-themed restaurant group, my client Aasia Baig asked my company to redesign everything except for the logo – but the logo was using a font from the wrong era. Rather than redesign it, I suggested a subtle tweak, by using a font from the correct era.

Before

After

This vastly improved the logo and made the rest of the redesign look better as a result. The font we chose had the added benefit of increasing legibility at small sizes and from a distance.

Aasia was amazed:

> 'I thought I didn't need to change the logo, but I was too close. A fresh pair of eyes was just what I needed. Once it was "cleaned up" it looked so much better!'

If you are thinking of engaging a new designer or agency, asking them to do a branding assessment will be a good way of seeing if you like how they think and if what they say makes sense.

Do you feel that they are sensitive to the amount of work that needs doing balanced with your business goals, current brand equity, timings and budgetary considerations – or not?

Case study: Antoinette Oglethorpe

Antoinette Oglethorpe had been in business for five years when we met. She came to me for a new brochure, but we needed to conduct a branding assessment of her existing brand assets to get a better idea of where she was now and where we should go.

In her own words, 'The branding assessment was invaluable and concluded that our marketing collateral lacked any consistency or strategy. It needed to be more pulled together to better represent the company, and me. It provided an opportunity for self-reflection, asking questions of who we are, who we help, how we're different, where we want to go...'

As time was tight before the book launch, we developed an 'evolution, not a revolution' strategy to phase her new look in.

- The book design for *Grow Your Geeks* had to stay. Despite the green not being one of her brand colours, it had tested well with her target audience and had already been promoted on social media.

- We decided to keep the shape of her logo the same so Antoinette could just replace the old one easily on her website and presentations, until the full rebrand. This included redeveloping the AO roundel as, with her long name, it was a useful branding element when space was an issue.

- We swapped the logo's script font for a more modern, professional font.

- Her strapline 'Talent Development' was too vague so we changed that to the more impactful and descriptive 'Develop Leaders – Deliver Strategy – Drive Results'.

TALENT
DEVELOPMENT

LEADERSHIP

COACHING

MENTORING

MATTERS

CAREER

CONVERSATIONS

Before: a mish-mash of styles, colours, typefaces and textures. From top, L-R: logo, website, training pack, product icons and book (which we kept)

- We ditched the girly fuchsia and garish cyan in her brand palette for the sophisticated and more grown-up 'jewel' shades that Antoinette loved. We used the bright green of her book, added a rich purple and deep blue to denote authority and a jade green for growth and development. A similar grey and purple from her old palette maintained some continuity. Antoinette saw this new palette as 'vibrant and modern, yet professional and trustworthy'.

We kept her existing photography and added to it with stock imagery, unifying the images with a filter treatment. Over time, we rolled the rebrand out: business cards, infographics and icons, her website, training packs and brochures.

These changes transformed Antoinette's business:

'The rebrand enhanced my credibility. It added a sophistication, maturity and extra layer of professionalism to everything. My company had 'grown up' and I was playing at a higher level. My brand is now aligned with who I am, what I do and what I am saying. First impressions are stronger: clients compliment me on it. I feel I'm being offered more significant opportunities as a result. It's much easier to be confident selling a high-value package when it looks the part too.'

This case study shows you the power of branding, but critically, it also shows how a branding assessment gives you a road map to help you understand where you need to go.

Antoinette ⬙ Oglethorpe

DEVELOP LEADERS • DELIVER STRATEGY • DRIVE RESULTS

After: Antoinette's new brand palette incorporated the green of her book with sophisticated jewel tones.
From top and L-R: logo, business cards, new icon styling, book, training pack and brochures

Part 1 summary

In Part 1, we've looked at the emergence of the brand and defined brand, branding, and personal branding. We've also explored the three key business problems entrepreneurs encounter and how branding can help with all of them. The DoSaySee model illustrates why branding should be integral to building your business, and you now know how to conduct a branding assessment.

The core benefits of branding will help you:

- Gain visibility, recognition and cut-through in your industry

- Communicate your vision more clearly

- Look more professional, credible and successful

- Feel more confident to go for the business you really want

- Attract your ideal clients and inspire their confidence in you

- Create brand clarity for you and your target market

- Build an authentic brand that you and your market will love

- Save you and your team time and money

- Charge more and increase the value of your business

In Part 2, we're going to learn how to achieve all that through the VISION process. Buckle up and enjoy the ride...

Part 2
The VISION Process

Visualise ▸ Inner Brand ▸ Stand Out ▸ Image ▸ Output ▸ Nurture

The VISION Process

In Part 2 of the book, I am going to take you through my six-step VISION process. Clients tell me they not only learn a lot from it, but they also enjoy the process and gain clarity for their entire business as a result.

Design without strategy is like building a mansion without foundations, so note that the first three steps of the process are all about research. The VISION process will help you understand branding so you can harness its power and align it with your business strategy, visions, aspirations and goals. It will help you get your ideas out of your head and clarify your thinking so you can brief any creative with confidence. VISION will demystify the branding process for you and produce powerful results – creating a brand that connects and resonates with people on a deep, emotional level.

The six steps of the VISION process are:

- **Visualise**: your brand aspirations, your company vision and your customer vision

- **Inner Brand**: the non-visual heart and soul of your brand: values, personality and voice

- **Stand Out**: learn how to differentiate yourself from your competitors

- **Image**: choose the right type, colour and imagery for your brand

- **Output**: what to expect from a branding project

- **Nurture:** how to look after your brand once it is launched

In *The Creative Curve*, Allen Gannett describes our paradoxical need for the familiar and craving for novelty. The VISION process works as it combines inspiration from the aspirational brands you love, identifies the visual cues within your industry, and gathers new ideas from sources outside your industry to create branding that feels familiar and looks established, whilst also looking fresh and different from your competition.

VISION will lead to more meaningful conversations, understanding and collaboration between you and your designer, so together you will create branding that deeply resonates with your business and your customers.

'Every minute you spend in planning saves 10 minutes in execution; this gives you a 1,000% return on energy!'

Brian Tracy

The first step of the VISION process, 'Visualise', will give you a direction to head in for the rest of the process. In the next chapter, we will explore your:

- Five aspirational brands (FABs)
- Your vision
- Your customer's vision

So without further ado, let's go!

Visualise

'I believe that visualisation is one of the most powerful means of achieving personal goals.'

Harvey Mackay, businessman, author, columnist

You may find it difficult to imagine your new brand right now, so I've developed a 'fab' little exercise which takes you out of your business for a moment. It's so much easier for you to understand what you want when you look at established brands that you admire or aspire to be like. One client was gobsmacked when I asked her for her FABs. When I questioned why, a tad embarrassed, she admitted, *'No designer has ever asked me what I like before.'*

My turn to be shocked. *'But how can anyone create a brand you love if they don't even know what you like?'*

After she'd done the FAB exercise, she said it 'felt like therapy'. It was the first time she'd stopped to really focus on what she liked and wanted for her brand, rather than being caught up in the day-to-day running of her business.

The FAB exercise is the first step in improving communication between you and your designer. If you asked for 'a luxury brand', your designer's unique experiences will mean they probably have a completely different view on what 'luxury' looks like.

This is why business owners get disappointed when they think they've given a clear brief to their designer, yet don't receive what they were expecting. It's also why designers often feel none the wiser after reading a client brief, wondering for example, 'What do they mean by "luxurious but accessible"?' No designer is a mind reader!

The FAB Exercise

In this exercise, we're going to:

- Choose your FABs

- Identify why that brand appeals to you

- Analyse any recurring themes and what you can apply to your own brand

Choose five brands that you admire or aspire to be like from a business point of view. These are the brands that make you say, 'I'd love for my company to be like that because of the way they look/make me feel/ the customer experience/the messaging...'

This exercise really does demonstrate that your brand is not your logo. You'll most likely find that these FABs embody your aspirations for your own business brand on not just a visual, but also an emotional, experiential and values-based level.

Your FABs do not have to be in your sector. In fact, it's more interesting if some of them are not. If you want to stand out in your industry, looking outside of it is a sure-fire way to inject some fresh thinking into proceedings.

Why five aspirational brands? I've found that five just works right. Fewer and you don't get enough of a picture. More is overwhelming. An odd number means you can see any bias. Five keeps things focused. Oh, and if you have other decision makers in the business, make sure you agree on those five brands together (you don't get five each).

If you are rebranding an existing business, you may want to ask a partner and/or a couple of trusted clients which FABs they would choose for your company, as I did for my own company's rebrand. It was wonderfully enlightening to see how others saw my business, and I chose my business' final FABs entirely from their suggestions:

- **John Lewis**: great customer service, quality, trust, satisfaction guaranteed, ethical, people come first

- **Mini**: cute, sassy, moves fast, fun, iconic, timeless

- **Veuve Clicquot**: an affordable luxury that you deserve; a strong, stand out, feel-good brand; makes the buyer feel special, someone worth celebrating

- **Apple**: intelligent, cool, beautiful design, form and function, effortless user experience (UX), easy to understand, intuitive, just *works*; strong personal brand in the visionary Steve Jobs

- **Virgin**: disruptive, doing things differently, carving its own path, energetic, standing out, fun, cheeky; strong personal brand in the founder Sir Richard Branson

Once you've chosen your FABs, use your laptop/tablet to bring up their brand websites one by one. Collate relevant visuals on your digital mood board – the things that appeal to you about those brands. It could be the logo, typography, layouts, imagery, slogans, quotes, whole pages or elements. Three to five visuals per brand is plenty.

Now analyse the FAB elements you have just pinned. Start a 'Brand Notes' document either digitally or in a notebook (I prefer digital as it's easier to amend and share). Look at your mood board. For each brand in turn, note what it is that appeals or resonates most for you. Is it the visual? Logo? Typography? Colours? Photography? Illustrations? Infographics? Styling? Layout? Boldness? Fun? Modernity? Elegance? Or is it more the emotive aspects? What the brand stands for or means to you? How it makes you feel? The values? The brand personality? The brand message or voice? The customer experience?

Once you've completed this for all five brands, look through your notes. Are there any common themes coming through?

This exercise should give you a strong idea of your own company brand aspirations and identify which brand traits you would like to take forward into your business and communicate via your branding.

Hopefully, you found that a fun and enlightening exercise. There are more of those to come, so save your notes for now. We'll be needing them later.

Case study 1: Find Peace of Mind

Emily Macpherson wished to rebrand her independent financial planning company, Find Peace of Mind. After having a terrible experience herself, Emily had retrained as an independent financial advisor (IFA) as she never wanted anyone to go through what she had. Her big 'why' is helping people feel secure and safe around managing their finances so that they can relax and enjoy their lives.

Three of Emily's FABs were Method cleaning products, Innocent smoothies and Abel & Cole organic produce boxes. None were in her industry because Emily didn't want to be like other IFAs as she didn't find them inspirational or aspirational. As we analysed these brands, four trends emerged that Emily resonated with:

- These brands were honest, friendly, approachable

- They were ethical, environmentally and socially responsible

- They all had an uplifting use of colour

- They were doing things with a typically British quirkiness or whimsy

We worked to weave these aspects into her branding to tap into what she wanted to communicate about her brand. Emily talks about a Mindful Money Tree in her book, so we used colourful photographs of elements of nature (e.g. a bird's nest for her property finance service) coupled with quirky illustrations of people enjoying their lives, having found peace of mind.

Emily was thrilled with the final outcome.

Series of brochures for Find Peace of Mind

Case study 2: Fearless Business

By way of contrast, business coach Robin Waite *didn't* think outside of his own industry and cited five business coaches as his FABs when we worked on his rebrand.

Luckily, I knew Robin well enough to challenge his choices. I struggled to see what was aspirational about some of them – also, most of the coaches were American and Robin is very British. He also loved surfing and was quite free-spirited with a casual, approachable style. He wore Saltrock T-shirts, not shirts and hoodies, not jackets.

I asked him why he hadn't listed Saltrock as one of his FABs. He said he hadn't thought of it as relevant to this exercise - but his coaching group was called Fearless Business! I made the connection that business is just like surfing: catching the breaks; riding the waves; falling down and getting back up; feeling on top of the world when things go well but at risk of drowning when they go badly.

The Fearless branding ended up taking its inspiration from the world of surfing. This not only injected real personality, energy and authenticity into the brand, it made it - and Robin - stand out from the competition.

He and his Fearless 'crew' felt far more connected to the new identity as a result. Robin loves his new brand so much, he got Fearless T-shirts made up, wears them every day, and his Saltrock ones have gone to the charity shop.

Some of the Fearless graphics for Robin's rebrand and one very happy client!

Your vision

Now it's time to turn back to your company. First, we'll look at your vision, and then we'll explore your customer's vision. The rest of the VISION process will bring these two visions together to create a brand that resonates for both.

Whilst it's crucial to build a brand that appeals to your target audience, this is *your* company, *your* livelihood. It represents a huge part of who you are, and with any luck, you'll be living and breathing this company for a while, so you have got to *love* your branding. If you feel proud of your brand and if your branding inspires you every day and aligns with your business goals, that makes it all the more powerful.

Time to add to those brand notes:

- Where are you now with your company?

- What's your vision and ambition over the next three to five years?

- What do you want to be known for? What is your brand promise? Why will people seek to work with you?

- What lasting difference do you want to make to your customers? To the world?

Your customer's vision

Now consider your ideal customer(s) – the decision makers and those who may influence the purchasing decision. You can continue in your brand notes whilst adding images to your mood board.

- Who is your ideal customer? What lifestyle do they lead and what brands do they admire? What gender and age are they? What do they do for a living? What do they read? Watch? Listen to? Drive? Wear? Where do they eat? Shop? Holiday?

- Where are they now in their lives? What are their problems that your business can help with?

- What are their aspirations and ambitions? What is their vision of how their life will look after they've spent time/money with you?

- What lasting difference will you make to their world?

Some of these are similar to questions relating to your vision, but I'm encouraging you to see things from your customers' point of view this time. Everyone who buys something is trying to fix a problem or fulfil a need, although it may not be obvious or identified as yet.

Even the guy who buys a new Ferrari has a problem. It may be a status thing: he was bullied at school and now needs people to see how successful he is. He may be lonely, trying to get noticed, win friends or attract the woman of his dreams. He may be insecure or trying to overcompensate for other areas of his life. Branding and brand messages focusing on the buyer's status and exciting life will resonate powerfully for him.

Remember that it doesn't matter if you are selling business-to-business (B2B) or business-to-consumer (B2C) – you are communicating human-to-human. Start looking deeply at why people may buy from you. If you can tap into a deep-rooted need in your customer that they didn't even know they had, that's incredibly powerful.

I remember being first-time pregnant and waddling around The Baby Show in London with my then-boyfriend, Andy. Blissfully unaware of all the baby paraphernalia that I'd have to cart around with me, I had naïve visions of just wearing my baby in a sling.

Then I spotted a mother wheeling an amazing space-age pushchair-thing along. I asked Andy to run after her (as I couldn't) to find out what it was.

We found the Stokke stand and asked for a demonstration of the travel system (for that's what the pushchair-thing was called). The assistant was showing us all the features, but I got distracted and mesmerised by the video playing on loop.

It showed the Stokke positioning the child so they got to see more of the world out of bus windows, over walls and shop counters. Better still, the child could be positioned to face their parent, boosting their interaction and communication skills. Adults would chat to the beaming child in the Stokke whilst kids in normal pushchairs languished at knee height, bored and mostly ignored. As if that wasn't enough, the amazing Stokke was shown protecting its precious cargo above exhaust fumes, cigarette smokers and wet, snuffling canines.

A pushchair – sorry *travel system* – that would make our child happier, cleverer and safer? We signed up on the spot.

Interestingly, the Stokke appealed to me first because of how it looked, then the video spoke to me and tapped into my until-then unidentified need to protect and develop my children, and only once we used it did we discover how clever it really was. See, Say, Do in that order.

Did Stokke deliver on its brand promise?

I guess people have always commented on how eloquent my boys are, so it must have helped, all the lovely chats I'd had with them. I was quite heartbroken when we finally had to sell it and I'm still a passionate brand advocate for Stokke and a loyal fan for life.

Case study: Slept Like a Baby

Shaleena's company Slept Like a Baby sells blackout blinds. Rarely a pleasurable or luxury purchase, they tend to be bought by shift-workers and parents who want to help their children get to sleep more easily, especially in the summer months and for daytime naps. They are seen as an essential product, their appearance often being secondary to their function.

Shaleena wanted to change that and focus on the baby-care sector and interior design space with the upper end of her range. These blinds are customised so buyers can have their child's name applied and/or theme the blinds to their room. She also provides beautifully custom-embroidered and sequinned blackout blinds for grown-ups' rooms.

I encouraged Shaleena to focus her branding not on the blinds' features (which probably don't vary much from those of her competitors), but around the life transformation that her products bring – hence her company name. The obvious product benefit that anyone in this space may first focus on is better sleep, but what does better sleep for baby actually *mean*?

Better sleep means a happier baby. Better sleep aids baby's learning and development. Better sleep for baby also means the parents sleep better, which gives them increased energy and makes them feel like they can cope with the day. This, in turn, makes them feel like better parents, workers, partners, friends. A happier, healthier and cleverer family from just buying blackout blinds? Sold!

We've now completed the first part of the VISION process.

Congratulations! The rest of the process will bring both your and your customers' visions together to create branding that communicates your company ambition and speaks to the vision, passions, dreams and latent desires of your ideal customers.

Inner Brand

'Define what your brand stands for, its core values and tone of voice, and then communicate consistently in those terms.'

Simon Mainwaring, brand futurist, global keynote speaker, author

The second stage of the VISION process is what I have called the Inner Brand. This is everything which is non-visual; the heart and soul of your company; its:

- Brand values
- Brand personality
- Brand voice

Tapping into people's beliefs to make an emotional connection will create brand passion and loyalty to carry your company through its highs and lows.

As Howard Shultz, CEO of Starbucks, said:

> *'If people believe they share values with a company, they will stay loyal to the brand.'*

I'm a straight-talking northerner, but I got a bit emotional when I worked through this section for my company's rebrand, and I've had clients choke up too with the revelation of what's truly important to them in their businesses.

Once you have defined your Inner Brand, it will give you amazing clarity, help your team stay on track, help you make the right decisions and communicate more clearly through every aspect of the business.

Brand values

Your company's brand values sit at the core of your business These are the unwavering, non-negotiable beliefs that drive every single one of your company's behaviours, providing clear guidance on how you and your team act daily.

Coupled with your vision, your values underpin everything your brand stands for, like the roots of a tree, and influence how it grows from the ground up.

For your customers, your brand values are the thing that will get them *here* (thumps chest). When communicated as part of your branding, your values will connect your customers with your company and brand on a much deeper level. Values can turn customers into loyal brand fans and passionate advocates.

Defining your company values

It is highly unlikely you, as an entrepreneur, will have started a company with values opposite to your own, so a good place to start is your personal values. The values of your FABs are also likely to be aligned with your own brand aspirations.

Defining your company values will take some thought, reflection and perhaps discussion with your team and clients. Even if it's only you in your business right now, this step is vital to growing a solid brand and scaling your business with the right people in your team.

You don't need many values – three to seven is about right. They should be easy to remember and follow for the whole team – a positive set of guidelines to live by, not a restrictive set of rules.

Input and buy-in from your team members are vital if you want them to embrace these values too. In fact, for my company's rebrand, I asked my team and a few trusted clients what they thought the values should be, why they loved working for or with us.

Their responses made for heart-warming reading. One value which came up time and time again, though, was 'straight-talking'. I'd never considered this a value before; it's just the way I am, so I hadn't realised how much it meant to my clients. Perhaps they were tired of jargon; of yes-people who didn't question, challenge or enlighten them, so didn't get the results they wanted. Maybe my level of honesty, of not being afraid to speak up if a client suggested something that wasn't going to work, was refreshing.

My clients also said that I provided clarity and intelligent solutions. That they felt they were in safe hands. They loved how involved and educated they felt by the whole process. They enjoyed working with me. I ended up compiling my company values from what my clients and team members found valuable to them too.

Once you have your values, print them out on A3 sheets to pin up on the office walls. Create a screensaver or desktop image showing them. Look at them frequently, act on them. At the start of my team meetings, I ask everyone to tell a real-life story that demonstrates one of our values. That way, I ensure they stay relevant, part of everyday actions, rather than a forgotten piece of paper.

A recent prospect wanted to book a One-Day Branding Workshop with me, but she needed to bring her toddler and baby to the initial meeting. As we chatted, she revealed they were all moving to Scotland the following week. I remarked that she looked remarkably relaxed about things and she smiled, admitting she was still in shock. The decision to move had all happened rather suddenly.

Minutes later, her baby managed to tip her tea everywhere. When I'd finished cleaning up the mess, I looked up to see big, fat tears rolling silently down her face. One of my company values is being people-focused, which made it easy to know what to do.

I hugged her and said that she needed to be kinder to herself, cut herself some slack. She had a nine-month-old baby on her lap and a toddler by her feet, so what on earth was she doing trying to sort her branding out at a time like this? I told her to focus on her little family, getting them settled into their new life. I wasn't going anywhere and her business, too, would wait.

She dried her eyes and hugged me gratefully as she left, asking me to send her the branding package anyway. I laughed and said I would do no such thing.

A couple of months later, a client of mine met this lady at an event. They realised they both knew me and my client said this lady 'couldn't speak highly enough' about how kind I'd been to her. Some might say I'd 'left money on the table', but staying true to my company's values and putting people first was more valuable to me.

My company values impact the smaller things, too. My social media manager found an article on innovative packaging designs. We often share inspirational design from other sources, but this packaging featured so much single-use plastic, it made me quite angry. I passionately believe we should all leave the planet in a better state than we found it – and that packaging designers have a huge responsibility for sustainability and reducing waste – so sharing this would not have aligned with our brand value of making a difference. We shared a post on innovative eco-friendly packaging design instead.

Values Exercise

So now to your values. Choose between three and seven and write or type them out in short action statements (we are/make/work/do…). Then expand a little on how those values might translate into actions.

For example: we are people-focused. We care about our clients' and each other's happiness, well-being and lives. We have fun, we are kind, we appreciate each other. We say thank you.

Documenting your brand values will help guide you, especially around the tougher decisions like turning away business, getting into partnerships and hiring people who align with them – or firing people who don't. What values would your company live and die by?

Brand personality

Let's give your company some personality. If your values are the 'heartfelt' core part of your brand, your brand personality is how those values are expressed and come to life. Your Inner Brand will become more tangible as we work through the personality section, and everything you produce in terms of brand assets will flow so much more easily.

Think of your brand personality as an imaginary trusted friend advising your ideal customer. What kind of person would share your company values and what kind of personality would they have so your clients would connect with, like, respect, trust and listen to them? Bear in mind that your brand personality may not share the personality of your ideal clients. If your customers are busy, stressed-out, high-level executives, your brand personality needs to be calm, reassuring, authoritative and knowledgeable.

Unlike defining your brand values, which often starts with your own values, you're best to separate your company's brand personality from your own. Or you may see your brand personality as a toned-down 'professional' or 'work' version of you. To illustrate, in real life I have a dark, satirical, filthy sense of humour. I get angry and passionate about political, social and ecological issues. I am enthusiastic so I tend to over-use exclamation marks in my texts. But I don't want those traits to seep into my company brand personality.

That doesn't mean my brand can't have a sense of humour. But it is toned down to a dry, intelligent or cheeky type of humour rather than my more edgy personal one. My company tends to steer clear of political issues, but my eco-warrior credentials frequently shine through loud and proud. Those exclamation marks are banished, lest they make my brand personality come across as immature or desperate. No one can take a B2B company seriously when it is *so* excitable *all* the time!!!!!!

My company personality (in case you are wondering) ended up being defined as friendly, positive, understanding, patient, collaborative, intelligent, honest and conscientious.

Personality Exercise

Here are some personality traits to get you started. Some of the words may be similar to your brand values, but how do those values present themselves in the behaviour of your company? That's your brand personality. Check back to your FABs again, too. Do they share any of your brand personality traits?

Choose no more than five to eight personality traits for your brand. Many more will be hard to communicate fully in your branding and marketing.

Finally, list five personality traits that you would not want associated with your brand. These are incredibly useful to prevent you and your team going off-piste with content. This step is especially vital for any copywriters or social media specialists who work with you.

Adventurous	☐	Independent	☐	Pure, innocent	☐
Approachable, friendly	☐	Informative, analytical	☐	Rebellious, wild	☐
Authoritative	☐	Inspirational	☐	Reliable, dependable	☐
Brash, loud	☐	Intelligent, advisory	☐	Responsible	☐
Calming, reassuring	☐	Irreverent, playful	☐	Romantic	☐
Chic, stylish, elegant	☐	Joyous, happy	☐	Sensual, intimate	☐
Confident	☐	Knowledgeable, wise	☐	Serious	☐
Corporate	☐	Leader	☐	Simple	☐
Courageous, bold, brave	☐	Light-hearted, humorous	☐	Sophisticated	☐
Creative	☐	Loyal	☐	Spiritual	☐
Direct, clear, straight-talking	☐	Luxurious, extravagant	☐	Strong, powerful	☐
Disruptive	☐	Masculine	☐	Supportive	☐
Empowering	☐	Mischievous	☐	Thoughtful	☐
Energetic, dynamic, exciting	☐	Modern, new	☐	Traditional	☐
Environmental, ethical	☐	Non-conformist	☐	Transformational	☐
Established, experienced	☐	Nostalgic	☐	Trendy, cool	☐
Family-friendly or focused	☐	Nurturing, maternal	☐	Trustworthy, honest	☐
Feminine	☐	Optimistic, positive	☐	Understanding	☐
Fun, funny	☐	Passionate	☐	Visionary	☐
Helpful, giving, caring, selfless	☐	Pioneering	☐	Warm	☐
Idealistic	☐	Prestigious, aspirational, elite	☐	Wholesome, natural	☐
Imaginative	☐	Professional	☐	Young, youthful	☐

Case study: Picture of Happiness

Yvonne James, founder of Picture of Happiness, really struggled with the Inner Brand exercise at first. One of her brand personality traits, she thought, should be 'kooky', because she considered herself to be kooky.

I explained that maybe her clients (brides-to-be and their families) are not looking for a 'kooky' solution for their big day or event, especially if they are stressed out already. What they need is a brand that is calm, reassuring, professional, knowledgeable and reliable. Of course, when they meet Yvonne, they discover her sweet nature and kookiness are totally charming – but it's not what her core clients would look for in their supplier, so it shouldn't be a part of the brand personality.

That's the second part of your Inner Brand completed. Great work! Your brand values and personality will now help you establish your brand voice.

Brand voice

Your branding helps you look great and communicate clearly with your target audience. Your brand voice should naturally evolve from and align with your brand values and personality. If your brand was a person talking to your ideal customer, and that person had your brand values and personality, how would they talk? What vocabulary would they use? What tone would they take?

Consider your target audience. Sleep-deprived new parent? Stressed-out, busy executive woman? Out-of-shape forty-something man? The brand voice, tone and vocabulary will be different for each.

My company brand is (among other things) intelligent, straight-talking, positive, approachable and knowledgeable. My clients are time-pressured and need clarity and to look the part, so brand content focuses on the positive transformations my company makes. My team and I seek to help our clients understand what they find complex with simple language, short words, short sentences and no jargon.

Voice Exercise

Speak into your phone's recorder about what your company does, and then listen back and write down key words that you use in your speech. Alternatively, get someone to role-play an ideal client, ask you questions and record your answers. Also list the banned words you would never use in your marketing.

Sarah is founder of The Independent Mamas, an online hub for single mothers. We created her brand's 'best friend/big sister' personality to be understanding, listening and empathetic, but also practical and no-nonsense. The type of woman who would not allow you to wallow in self-pity. So in came language such as 'take action', 'stop', 'start'; out went softer, fluffier words more suited to a spa brochure ('re-energise', 'revive'). This gave Sarah so much more clarity on how to write her copy.

Once you've got your brand voice, here are a few more tips for kick-ass copy.

- **Write or speak directly to one client** (i.e. address 'you' not 'everyone'). The late, great Sir Terry Wogan was once asked how he'd managed to achieve the most listened-to radio show in Europe with over eight million listeners. He famously responded that he only ever spoke to one person.

- **As with your holiday packing, write your copy, then halve it.** Cut the cr*p and get to the point. We all know that you're the expert and passionate about what you do, but your time-poor clients don't want or need to know it all. Just give them enough to whet their appetite and take action.

- **Don't go on about how brilliant your product or service is**. People only care about what's in it for them. Tell your customer how it will make their life better, how *they* will feel. Your reader's brain is quick-firing, 'What's this about? Why should I buy this? Why buy from you? What will you do for me? How do I know this will work? What do I do now?' Answer those questions.

- **Ask your clients why they love working with you** and use phrases from their testimonials. Identify key words that resonate with your brand personality and incorporate those into your brand voice. Then your marketing will literally be speaking your clients' language.

- **Make it easy to read.** Plain English, short words, short sentences. Real-life language helps people better understand how you can help them. Keeping things simple also reassures clients that working with you will be easy. A general tip is to write for an eleven-year-old – yes, even in business communications. If you don't have an eleven-year-old handy, use the free readability-checker at www.thewriter.com. This chapter has a reading age of twelve.

- **Avoid all business 'BS'** and technical or bamboozling industry jargon. It doesn't make you look clever. It confuses and irritates readers, and you can end up sounding a bit pompous. If no one can understand what you're saying, how will they know how awesome your offering is? www.bullshitbingo.net is a bit of fun, but it does give you a whole list of words to avoid peppering your copy with.

- **Proofread!** Make sure your spelling and punctuation are on point. If you don't care enough to get the basics right for your own company, potential customers may well wonder about your standards elsewhere. *Eats, Shoots and Leaves* by Lynne Truss is a brilliantly funny book about punctuation and grammar. The Plain English Campaign will also proofread and edit your copy for you.

- **Should copy be in the first or third person?** Go back to your brand values and brand personality. How do your industry competitors and aspirational brands communicate?

Generally, I would say:

Third person = position of authority and knowledge, i.e. 'this person is an expert'

First person = position of empathy and understanding, i.e. 'I understand your problem'

If you've built your business around a problem you've personally experienced, and your copy is your story, write it in the first person. Anna Burrows of *The Coeliac Lifestyle* is building a community of fellow coeliacs. Her relationship with consumers is direct as she is coming into their lives and kitchens, albeit virtually, so it's an intimate, personal one. She relates to and shares her community's problems, so she uses the first person.

Alexander Seery of *Shifts to Success* is building a global business with a team of mentors delivering his course with him. The information on the mentors is written in the third person, as his company is introducing them all to his clients and establishing their positions of authority.

If it's your biography on the back of your book jacket or brochure, it's standard to write in the third person to establish authority, but if, say, you're introducing yourself on your website in your 'about us' section, it may sound more approachable and 'real' to write in the first person. Some people feel it's easier to list all their achievements in the third person on their site (like someone else wrote it rather than themselves) and that's fine too. Just be mindful that this is an authoritative tactic, so if your brand personality isn't that way inclined, it may not be the most appropriate voice for you.

You're now a third of the way through the VISION process and have defined a really important part of your branding in your Inner Brand values, personality and voice. These non-visual elements will help you create a far more meaningful brand. They will also help clarify your branding journey and make subsequent decisions much easier as you work through the rest of the book.

The lasting legacy of the Inner Brand is that long after you have finished your branding project, it will guide you and your team in your business every day, and give your customers a reason to fall in love at first sight with, and stay lifelong loyal to, your brand.

Case study: Mark Bowden

Mark Bowden was re-focusing his hypnotherapy business towards performance and mindset coaching for professional footballers. He had written a book about it but was struggling with the title, despite multiple suggestions from his network, coaches and publisher.

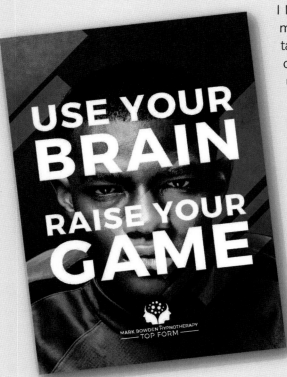

I listened as he ran the suggestions by me. They were all quite long and wordy, talking about accessing the latent power of the mind, tapping into potential by unleashing your brainpower, harnessing the power of the brain to enhance your performance… but this was a book aimed at footballers.

The right brand voice for this target audience needed to be the sort of motivational language you'd hear in the locker room before a match, using short, sharp and punchy words.

As I sipped my hot chocolate, inspiration struck. Mark loved the title so much, we also used it for his brochure and it became the strapline for his subsequent rebrand.

Stand Out

'The world accommodates you for fitting in, but only rewards you for standing out.'

Matshona Dhliwayo, philosopher, entrepreneur and author

Standing out helps you get noticed – and getting noticed is vital for success. If you are not noticed in the first few seconds, you are not visible enough and your customers will be drawn to your better-looking competitors, despite all your efforts. Not being visible enough to get noticed will render you as good as invisible.

Grabbing attention and differentiating your company from your competitors is key to developing a recognisable and memorable brand. Showing up with consistency then builds familiarity, familiarity builds trust, and that is how you develop a lasting relationship with your clients. In this chapter we will look at three key ways to help you Stand Out and be more memorable:

- Your company name

- Your strapline

- Competitor and market analysis

Company name

What's in a name? As for a baby, choosing your company name needs some serious consideration. Mergers, acquisitions or complete rebrands aside, your company name will likely exist for its lifetime.

Your company name is the first way you will make an impact in your industry and an easy way to stand out and be memorable. If you have an existing business name you are happy with, then great – you can skip this bit. The only caveat is that if you are using your own name as your company name, do consider your exit strategy if you ever want to sell the company in the future. Also, consider that a name other than your own name will make your company look bigger than just you.

Even if you've been established a while, if you need to take your business to the next level, don't be afraid to change your company name as part of your rebrand. Of course, you need to get it right this time. One name change is forgivable, but if you continuously chop and change, things will soon get expensive, look a bit suspicious and totally confuse your customers.

Invite stakeholders or a trusted friend/partner to help. Crack open a bottle of wine if it gets the creative juices flowing.

- Take a large piece of paper and a marker (or fire up a screen)

- Note down what you do first and who you do it for, either in the centre of the page or the top of a list, whatever works for you

- Ask someone to 'interview' you and ask questions

- Talk about how and why you started the business, your methodology, your customer problems, why they are really buying from you, the transformation you bring to their lives

- List or 'mind map' all the pertinent words and phrases that arise

- Revisit your Inner Brand work whilst you're brainstorming

A frequent lament from my clients is: 'All the good names are taken!' It may seem that way as you come up with the obvious ideas that everyone else has thought of too. Keep pushing through and you'll end up with a name that's more creative than theirs.

Ways of naming your business

Name by 'desire' e.g. SlimFast, Clean & Clear, easyJet. These brand names describe what the company does, the experience, unique selling point (USP), benefit or value it brings; they're selling the dream.

I love a 'Ronseal' (does-exactly-what-it-says-on-the-tin) kind of name. Anything that helps customers understand in seconds why they should work with you means your business name is working harder for you, so take all the help you can get. Think back to your vision, the solutions you provide and the transformation you bring to your customers' lives, as I did when I helped name wedding planning company, MyOhMy Weddings.

Name by problem e.g. Weightwatchers, Rentokil, No More Nails. These brand names are tapping into the customer's pain points and may describe the problem they are fixing. Because I'm a happy, optimistic kinda gal, I prefer to focus on positive outcomes rather than problems, but this is still a valid route.

Use alliteration e.g. Fitness First, American Airlines, Dunkin' Donuts. Brand names that have words starting with the same letters are more memorable and trip off the tongue nicely. I did this for my client, Shifts to Success.

Own a word out of context e.g. Apple, Amazon, Pandora. It will be harder to trademark or establish a 'real word' as a brand name, you will need to work harder on your Google search and you will need to educate the market as to what you do. Remember that most of these big brands have had decades and spent billions to achieve their level of brand awareness, recognition and understanding, but if you are in a crowded marketplace and all the obvious words are taken, this is a great way to stand out in your industry, as I did for ei8ht Leadership Coaching.

Deliberately misspell a real word e.g. Google,[1] Krispy Kreme, Flickr. This is a great way to have a unique name and a popular strategy, especially when your favourite words have been taken. It's also easier to trademark. Be prepared to have to spell out your brand name and for people to mistype it until you get well-known. You can, of course, use social media and search terms to raise awareness and drive traffic to your website.

Invent a word e.g. IKEA (from the initials of founder Ingvar Kamprad plus the first letter of the property, Elmtaryd, and the village he grew up in, Agunnaryd), Cisco (a shortened version of San Francisco), LEGO (a contraction of *leg godt*

---

1   A 'googol' is the number 1 with 100 zeros after it, alluding to the number of possibilities on the internet.

which means 'play well' in Danish). Yes, you may need to work a bit harder to educate the market on what you do, but the uniqueness will be yours and you can create a really meaningful name. My client Rebecca Godfrey named her company Etheo after her two sons Ethan and Theo – a lovely, constant reminder for her of why she went into business.

Use your initials e.g. IKEA (again), BMW (Bavarian Motor Works) or H&M (Hennes and Mauritz). This is probably the one where it's the hardest to make a meaningful or emotive connection with your target customer, especially without the benefits of time and money.

Try a word mash e.g. Microsoft (microcomputers + software), Groupon (group + coupon), LEGO (again). This is where you choose two words that describe your product, service or business idea and mash them together to make a new word. These are pretty cool, and if you get a good one, it will help people understand what you do *and* be unique and memorable too.

Take global inspiration e.g. Uber, Reebok (an African antelope), Nike (Greek for 'Goddess of Victory'). Do check the word's meaning and make sure it doesn't have any negative connotations in other markets you may wish to enter. You may have read of the Vauxhall Nova bombing in Spain because *no va* means 'doesn't go/work' in Spanish. Apparently, this is just an old marketers' tale, but it proves my point so we'll ignore the fact it's not true just this once.

Whatever method you use, remember:

- No idea is a bad idea. Get them all out of your head.

- Use an online dictionary and thesaurus to find alternative words.

- Keep it simple, interesting, meaningful and/or memorable. Don't try to be too clever.

- If you have visions of expanding into other markets in the future, make sure the name is wide-reaching enough to cope.

- Say it out loud. Check it makes sense to others, doesn't sound weird and is easy to pronounce. If people can't say your brand name, it can affect word-of-mouth recommendations.

- Write your business name down without spaces to avoid unfortunate URLs like 'penisland.com', 'therapist.com' or 'molestationnursery.com' (for real!).

- Check availability of any names that 'stick' via Companies House. There might be another company registered with the same name but in a different industry, so add another word to make it unique.

- Same applies for your website – you may add a word or choose a different dot-suffix to secure the URL. A dot-com address is still desirable, but dot-co-dot-uk is perfectly fine if your business is staying UK-based. Dot-global is getting popular and makes your company seem huge from the start, but depending on your business, consider others like dot-club or dot-life.

- Trademark your brand name and logo via the Intellectual Property Office on www.gov.uk/how-to-register-a-trade-mark. Also, read the section on protecting your IP in the Nurture chapter. This is vital if you are planning on scaling your business.

Lastly, especially if you took my tip on the wine (*cough*), do sleep on any name you decide and don't register it until the next day, no matter how much you love it!

Case study: Shifts to Success

Ex-detention custody officer turned successful property developer Alexander Seery wanted to help other police officers who wished to leave the force and change their lives for the better by becoming entrepreneurs too. I knew I wanted to work with him, but I spent the next forty minutes plucking up the courage to admit that I didn't like his business name, Escape the Shifts.

It was a risky strategy: Alex had already registered the business name, bought the URL, published videos and his friends loved it!

I explained that 'Escape the Shifts' was far too negative. It talked about running away from the problem rather than the positive transformation his company would bring into people's lives. I'd been making notes as Alex had talked and suggested a new company name: Shifts to Success.

This was much more positive, with a double-layered meaning. The new name not only talked about transitioning from a life of shift-work to business success, it also referred to the incremental steps or shifts needed to attain that success. It named the company by desire, used alliteration, was easy to spell, say and understand. The name appeared to also be available.

Tick, tick, tick, tick, BOOM! It was at that point that Alex decided he wanted to work with me. Crucially, Shifts to Success is also a name that is broad enough to take the company beyond the police force.

Strapline

Once you've secured your company name, you can start looking at your strapline (or tagline). Whilst you were working on naming your business, you'll have generated a lot of relevant words that didn't make the final cut. Don't waste them. Add them to your brand voice vocabulary if you can use them in your content. They will also be useful as you think about your strapline.

What is a strapline? Do you really need one? Your strapline is a short, powerful phrase that is paired with your company name to communicate something extra and meaningful about your offering. It may form part of your logo and/or may be used separately.

Think about your strapline from the customer's point of view. What is your offering or promise to them? This could be something that describes your business, the difference you make, an uplifting or motivational statement or why customers might choose or value you.

Your strapline is a powerful marketing and brand positioning tool. In seconds, it gives you:

- Differentiation, helping you stand out from your competitors
- A clear and memorable promise to potential customers
- A hook to help customers feel an affinity with your brand

Whilst it's not essential to have a strapline, why wouldn't you want to take any opportunity to tell people a bit more about your company? It's a quick and easy way to stand out and make a powerful impact in prospects' minds, so it would be a missed opportunity not to have one.

A strapline stays constant, as opposed to a slogan, which is a line that may change tactically for a campaign. When you're brainstorming straplines, save any rejects as potential slogans for campaigns in the future.

A strapline needs to be memorable. Short and punchy action words have the most power. Generally, I recommend three to four words, or no more than eight syllables as optimum. It can be a phrase, like my client Invincible Apparel's 'X-shaped Fashion that Fits', or three separate words (the power of three), as with ei8ht Leadership Coaching's 'Liberate. Motivate. Elevate.' The strapline for Shifts to Success is 'Break out. Make the change. Live your life.' These words take the customer on a journey and articulate the real value of working with the company – the customer vision and brand promise in just a few syllables.

Here are a few famous examples to inspire you further:

Nike – *Just do it.* Empowering, positive, gender-neutral, powerful. This is about an attitude rather than a particular sport or product, which allows for any amount of future diversification.

L'Oréal – *Because you're worth it.* Another empowering strapline, delivered by a host of internationally famous, glamorous spokeswomen. L'Oréal may be a mass-market brand, but its positioning is highly aspirational, implying that its products will make you feel a million dollars.

Gillette – *The best a man can get.* The brand was obviously promising the best shave, but the implication was always that Gillette would also help a man snag a gorgeous girlfriend. In 2019, Gillette started to evolve its brand in the wake of the #metoo movement. It hasn't changed its strapline but has created a slogan for a campaign around 'The best men can be', showing men calling out sexism and championing equality. This brave move went viral, but divided opinion and alienated some of the brand's core audience.

De Beers – *A diamond is forever*. A brand promise that speaks not just of everlasting love, but of an heirloom which can be passed on to your children, and their children too. Suddenly spending all those thousands feels like an investment.

Apple – *Think different*. Yes, if you're British, it should be 'Think differently' and it was actually an advertising slogan, not a strapline, but this one has endured and became iconic in itself as it is aspirational, visionary, exciting, rebellious, timeless and deeply aligned with Apple's company and brand strategy.

Competitor and market analysis

Analysing your industry and indirect competitors' logos is a vital step to creating a stand out brand. You have to know what you're up against if you're going to outperform the competition. I love this part of the VISION process because it's immensely reassuring that, with a bit of effort, you can easily look better than the rest. It's also at this stage when my clients begin to really understand what they like and want.

Of course, unless you run a well-known fashion or luxury label, people don't choose your product or service for the logo. But we will start with the logo because that's how people first recognise a company.

In this section, we will explore three key areas for visual understanding and inspiration:

- Your competition and related industries

- Your FABs

- Other sources of visual inspiration

Your competition and related industries

Type your industry sector and related industry sectors with the word 'logos' into the Google search-box and click the word 'Images' in your search options when you get the results. Use the words that customers might search for if they were looking for your company. For example, if you're in the property market, try 'estate agent logos', 'lettings agents company logos', 'mortgage lender company logos', etc. Screengrab whole page results or select individual logos and images that catch your eye (good or bad). Add them to your mood board and annotate them if it helps.

Your FABs

Look back at your FABs and note if there is anything visual about them that you like. Is it the typestyles? The colours? The imagery? Are the logos cool and sophisticated or bold and colourful? What are the layouts like? Are there any similarities or trends? No one chooses their FABs based on visuals alone, but it's worth saving and noting any visual elements you do like from them right now, and perhaps even exploring other great brands in your FAB industries.

Other sources of visual inspiration

Looking for inspiration outside your field is the best way to create something different within it. Inspiration can come from anywhere. It depends on what image you want to go for or what your USP may be, e.g. for an executive women's coach in New York, I looked at 'New York fashion designers' and 'women's magazines' to make her brand stand out from her competition. Add any visuals that appeal to your board.

This part of the Stand Out task is my favourite because everything starts falling into place. It shows you what else is out there. You will be able to identify the visual norms and clichés in your industry. For example, in the wedding industry, there are a lot of swirly script typefaces, golds and soft pink colours and images of flowers, rings and hearts. Organic companies are green and brown with leaves, plants, trees and recycled brown paper or card. There are a lot of houses, rooves and keys in the property industry.

Of course, visual languages are an established shortcut to communicating with your target market, so you don't have to reject every industry norm going. But changing even one element (type, colour or imagery) to avoid the full-on cliché can visually communicate a point of difference and help you stand out from your competitors. It's the quickest way to discover what you like and don't like. Once you've collated imagery from your industry, related industries, FABs and other sources, look at them as a whole and consider:

- What styles of typeface do you and don't you like?

- Which colours work for you and which ones don't?

- What about the imagery?

Refer back to your FABs and brand notes to see if there are any recurring themes there too. Which of your chosen visuals align in look and feel to the brand you are trying to build? Discuss with your designer what works and what doesn't for you and your industry, and the clichés you might want to avoid.

It prevents you ending up with a 'copycat' logo. Imitation may be the sincerest form of flattery, but when it comes to logos, you are wandering into potential court-case territory, especially if the competitor is bigger than you are. If you're serious about your business, you'll need something unique that you can trademark and protect (see also the section on protecting your IP in the Nurture chapter).

Stand out will help you and your designer know what's out there and prevent copycat solutions. Another check for proposed design(s) is to drag a JPEG into your Google image finder box for a 'reverse image' search. This will bring up images similar to your logo. Try the whole logo, the name part of the logo and the symbol or image separately.

It helps you to brief your brand designer with more clarity. You may not be able to describe exactly what you want – and you may not know what you like until you see it. But why waste your money and your designer's time generating a load of ideas you're not going to buy? There are thousands of designers who've already done that for you on the web – so use those images to have an open and honest discussion with your designer, getting to know and understand each other in the process. In going through the stand out stage and learning more about what you love and don't love, you and your designer can both agree a creative direction and clarify the brief before they start designing.

Case study: Buddy's Beats

Ashley Webber is a musician. His company, Buddy's Beats, teaches clients to play a favourite song on guitar or keyboard so they can wow their family and friends at a special event.

In the stand out phase, Ashley and I started by looking for inspiration within his industry, searching through 'music school' and 'music teacher' logos. We saw all the usual clichés – notes, clefs, guitars, plectrums, speakers, keyboards – and not much else. So uninspiring!

We needed to think outside of this beatbox. Potential customers needed to feel excited about Ashley's offering, so we thought back to the customer vision. Why would they want to do this?

They wanted to fulfil a lifelong ambition. For once in their lives, for one night only, live on stage, they wanted to wield an axe, strut the stage, surprise and impress their adoring crowd. They wanted to feel like a rock star for the day.

So we turned to the music greats for inspiration, collating iconic band logos from the Beatles and The Who to The White Stripes, plus music brands like Fender and Gibson.

The result was a logo that, although new, energetic and unique, looked strangely familiar because it took visual cues from the bands we'd grown up with – tapping into that human paradox of craving novelty but loving the familiar.

From top, L-R: logo,
business cards,
plectrums, social
media and button
badge icon, Buddy in
his branded tee

You're halfway through the VISION process! So far we've Visualised: analysed your FABs, defined your three- to five-year vision and your customer's vision. We have developed your Inner Brand and how that will help your customers feel more connected to your brand. In Stand Out, we have discovered three ways branding can help you differentiate your company:

- Your company name
- Your strapline
- Competitor and market analysis

You'll now have a better idea of what works and doesn't work for you and gathered fresh ideas and inspiration from outside your industry. You will have built a strong foundation for your brand and branding and will hopefully feel a lot more confidence and clarity around briefing a designer whilst you move through the second design-led half of VISION: 'Image', 'Output' and 'Nurture'.

Image

'Design is thinking made visual.'

Saul Bass, designer, Oscar-winning film-maker

The fourth step of the VISION process, image, is where all that thinking and research becomes visual and your brand's look finally starts to come together. This is the 'See' part of your 'DoSaySee' – the exciting bit. This section will help you understand the power and psychology of three key elements to create branding that truly represents and reflects the brand you're creating:

- Type
- Colour
- Imagery

Preparation and research are everything in the VISION process, so this is the time to engage with and take your designer through your mood board. Along with the information you have gathered so far, this fourth step will help you both decide the creative direction before any design is undertaken. My clients and I gain so much clarity by the end of the image stage that they often sign off their final approved logo from the first round of ideas.

If you haven't got a designer yet, we will take you through how to find one in Part 3.

Typography

There are over 100,000 typefaces,[1] each with its own distinctive personality, and each will give a different feel to your brand, so it's not enough to just choose your favourite.

The right typeface(s) will support your Inner Brand and help reinforce and communicate your brand message to your target audience on a powerful subconscious level.

Even before we bring colour and imagery in, and even if you think you know little about design, you can instantly see that the typeface choices for this fictional company are completely inappropriate. Choosing the wrong typeface can do untold damage to your brand.

CLEVER BRIGHT & RICH
Divorce Lawyers

---

1   Source *Just My Type*, Simon Garfield

Imagine if the Gucci logo was redesigned in Comic Sans. Would it still look luxurious and desirable?

GUCCI

GUCCI

Choosing the right brand typeface

With so many to choose from, I can't tell you here which typeface is absolutely right for your brand. Like people, each typeface has a different character to it, and subtle treatments can alter the feel of them, for example how far apart the letters are, what case they appear in (more on that later), what colour they appear in (more later), when they were designed (some are classics, others don't age well) and which other typefaces you pair them with.

What I can give you is a broad overview of the main type categories so you can understand the styles which may suit your brand personality and start an informed conversation with your designer.

Serif fonts

Serif typefaces have little strokes at the ends of the letters.

Serifs are some of the most versatile typefaces.

Top: Source Serif Variable, Bottom: Ratio Modern

- Books, newspapers and magazines were traditionally set with serif fonts. The 'feet' at the ends of the letters help our eye to scan lines of copy at greater speed.

- Serifs are versatile and can be used for logos, titles and copy.

- Serifs help brands appear professional, serious, established, traditional, learned and trustworthy, so are used by a lot of legal and accountancy firms and corporates.

- Serifs can look high-end, so may be used by luxury brands, hotels and wedding suppliers.

- Other serifs can make your brand look dated or old-fashioned – some serifs are more contemporary than others.

Sans-serif fonts

Sans-serif typefaces have no strokes at the ends of the letters.

'Sans' is French for 'without'.
They are as versatile as serifs.

Top: Source Sans Variable Black, Bottom: Azo Sans Thin Italic

- Sans-serifs are cleaner, simpler and more modern-looking than most serifs.

- Sans-serifs are as versatile as serifs and may be used for logos, titles and copy.

- Sans-serif typefaces can help brands look youthful, modern, contemporary, pure, open and/or friendly.

- Sans-serifs are used widely for all kinds of brands, but especially those targeting a younger demographic, or those connected with technology and progressive thinking. Thinner sans-serifs can be used to give a luxury look.

- Sans-serif fonts have simpler letter-shapes which render with more clarity on to small screens, so are used by all the social media platforms.

Contrasting sans-serifs with serif fonts adds visual interest and nuance, for example, if you wish to look modern *and* established.

Semi-serif fonts

Semi-serifs are a halfway house between serifs and sans-serifs.

They are characterised by a slight 'flourish' at the end of letters.

Top: Optima, Bottom: Khmer KN

- Semi-serifs sit between serifs and sans-serifs, characterised by a small 'kick', flare or flourish at the end of some or all of the letters
- Usually as versatile as serifs and sans-serifs
- Contrast these with sans-serif fonts

Script fonts

Script typefaces are best for display use only.

Do not use for copy and never in CAPITALS!

Top: Adage Script, Bottom: Edwardian Script

- Script fonts are decorative, more formal and 'floral', characterised by the flourishes and swirls a calligrapher might use for lettering, these have a sense of occasion.

- For display use only, e.g. logos, titles and social media images. Often used in the hospitality, events or wedding, 'traditional' or more female-targeted markets.

- Brands use script fonts to look classy, elegant and high-end.

- Beware, the wrong choice can be illegible or look old-fashioned.

- Do not use for copy and never use script fonts in capitals. Contrast with a simple serif or sans-serif for copy that needs to be read.

Handwritten/brush fonts

Handwritten typefaces can add a human touch to your brand communications.

Do not use brush scripts in copy, nor in CAPITALS.

Top: Huh Girls, Bottom: HelloScript

- Both are slightly looser, less formal and more contemporary versions of script fonts.

- Can make brands feel more spontaneous, elegant, feminine, personable, personal or playful.

- Use in moderation as for script fonts: logos, titles, social media.

- Beware, some of these fonts can make your brand look 'cheap', others are over-used. Choose a well-designed one that is not too common and make legibility a priority.

- Do not use for copy and never use script fonts in capitals.

- Use with a complementary serif or sans-serif font for contrast within a logo and for copy.

I personally feel that handwritten fonts have become a bit of a cliché for female-run/targeted businesses and motivational Instagram memes. It's harder to stand out if everyone in your industry is using a certain font, and you risk it dating your brand when it's not on-trend any more. Remember that your logo needs to have some longevity to it.

Decorative fonts

Decorative fonts are best kept for display.

They can come from any era.

Top: Sneakerscript, Bottom: Mostra Nuova

- Decorative fonts can be inspired by an era, e.g. Victorian, Art Deco, the 1970s; or cultural references, e.g. the Wild West, technology, graffiti, sci-fi. They can be 3D, coloured, patterned or textured.

- These are display fonts so use for logos or titles.

- Contrast with a simple serif or sans-serif for copy.

- Unless your business is linked to a certain era or cultural reference, some of these can look a bit 'novelty' so use sparingly for effect, e.g. for themed events.

Bespoke fonts

- It can be expensive to get a whole typeface designed, but for global brands like LEGO, Volkswagen and Google it saves millions in advertising and merchandise licensing fees.

- You may choose to have a unique logotype designed, like Coca Cola...

- Alternatively, a hack we often use to give clients a unique logo is to modify an existing typeface. The Google logotype is set in its own bespoke font, Product Sans, but looks a lot like a modified Futura font.

Google

Google

Google

Top: How the Google logo might look if it were set in Futura Medium

Middle: Futura Medium (red lines) overlaid on top of the real Google logo so you can see the difference. Note the more open and rotated 'e' - it makes the brand feel friendlier and happier

Bottom: The real Google logo

Here's a logo I created for IT company, Fluent Forward. We needed to make it look modern and dynamic, systems-driven but approachable, so we based the logo on two typefaces, BC Alphapipe and Century Gothic Bold. We then modified these to make them unique and give the meaning of the words more visual impact.

fluent**forward**

fluent**forward**

fluent**forward** ▶▶

Transforming Product Development Teams

Top: The unaltered typefaces

Middle: Kerning is adjusted (original spacing shown in blue) and alterations made to individual letters (shown in red)

Bottom: The finished logotype is now totally bespoke and unique

The 'fluent' was made more fluid by joining the letters together. The 'forward' was made more dynamic with a forward-leaning w, and the f and rs were angled a touch too. We also manually adjusted the spacing to even out the spacing between each letter, called kerning.

'Kerning is King!' One of our clients actually said that after he saw the difference it makes. Kerning is an art form and *vital* to give your logo professional polish. If something isn't looking 'right' or your logo looks a bit 'budget', check the kerning.

How many typefaces should my branding have?

Before we begin, in case you've ever wondered about the difference between typefaces and fonts, if Helvetica is the typeface (family name), Bold, Italic and Regular are the fonts (family members). But the terms are used pretty interchangeably these days.

The general recommendation is to use no more than three typefaces for your entire branding scheme. Of course, there are always brands that break the rules. We had so much fun breaking all the type rules with this wonderfully maximalist logo for interior design company, Quirk & Colour (right).

I generally use one or two typefaces for the logo and one for the strapline (which might be from the same family). You can mix up typestyles, e.g. a decorative logo font with a sans-serif strapline, but if one typeface is distinctive, keep the others simpler and more neutral to avoid visual overload and let the fancier one take centre-stage.

I try to use fonts from the same family as the logo for headings and copy, or at least ones that are complementary. My company only uses one typeface (Aktiv Grotesk), with different font weights, sizes and italics for visual interest.

There are millions of possible combinations, so your designer should help you choose typefaces or fonts to match your brand personality. For a professionally designed look, avoid the typefaces that come bundled with Microsoft Office, like Times New Roman, Arial, Helvetica and especially Comic Sans, possibly the most maligned font in the world. It's impossible to take any company seriously that uses Comic Sans.

Please note that asking your designer to share their fonts with you is legally piracy. There are some fonts available free online, but you may need to buy others. Your web designer may also need to purchase them for your website unless you have a suitable Google font match (these are free, but they don't match most Adobe fonts that your brand designer will likely use). Be aware of the licensing rights and that licence fees may increase if you are using your typefaces on sellable items.

Light, *Light Italic*
Regular, *Italic*
Medium, *Medium Italic*
Bold, ***Bold Italic***
X Bold, ***X Bold Italic***
Black, ***Black Italic***

abcdefghijklmnopqrstu vwxyzABCDEFGHIJKLM NOPQRSTUVWYZ.

abcdefghijklmnopqrstuvwxyz
ABCDEFGHIJKLMNOPQRSTUVWXYZ.

Aktiv Grotesk is a very versatile typeface.
The Adobe version here comes in no less than fourteen fonts (top)

However, this book is only set in three weights of Aktiv Grotesk throughout:
XBold for headings (centre), Light for copy (below) and Light Italic for captions (here)

What case is right for my logo?

When I start designing a logo for a client, I will show them their company name in a few different cases so they can see what a difference to the tone or mood this makes. Of course, the weight of font (bold, medium, light, etc), whether it's italicised or not, the colour and the combination of fonts will also make a difference, but choosing the right case is a start.

lower-case logos look more youthful, modern, approachable, friendly, non-threatening, feminine and/or gentle. Many technology brands use this tactic to feel more user-friendly *(1)*.

UPPERCASE logos can look authoritative, more masculine and stronger in 'bolder' typefaces, or elegant, designer and high-end in more refined ones *(2)*.

UPPER and lower-case logos are the way most people write names, so they are a popular option. They're professional, quietly confident and do not alienate any demographic, so are good for any brand with a broad appeal *(3)*.

Title Case logos have a capital letter at the start of every word. Traditional, smart, serious, intelligent, these have gravitas *(4)*.

camelCase logos are where a word is capitalised in the middle of the brand name to emphasise each word and aid legibility and/or pronunciation *(5)*.

mIXeD cAse logos give an eye-catching, quirky or eclectic vibe to your brand (see Quirk & Colour).

(1) **facebook** pepsi

(2) J O M A L O N E MAN CAVE
L O N D O N

(3) Google Microsoft

(4) Deutsche Bank [Z] The Telegraph

(5) ▶ YouTube iPhone

Refer back to your FABs and stand out research so you know what kind of feel you want and ask your designer to try out your company name in different cases, typefaces and weights to see which communicate your brand personality best.

I'm such a type geek, I could have easily written a whole book on typography alone, but for your sake, I'll stop. I have sneaked in some more tips on typesetting in the Brochure section in the Output chapter and the Jargon Buster, which will help you have an even more informed conversation with your designer.

Colour

In 2005, in Mason County Jail, Texas, Sheriff Clint Low decreed that everything in the prison should be pink: walls, bars, sheets, towels, jumpsuits and slippers. Amazingly, aggression levels plummeted and the fighting stopped – I guess it's hard to act the big man when you're dressed like a baby girl! Inmates also reported that they felt humiliated to be seen doing community service dressed in pink and didn't want to have to wear the outfits again. Reoffending rates dropped by an astonishing 70%.[2]

If colour can have such a powerful effect on hardened criminals, think how it could affect your customers. *Colour* has a deep psychological effect on our emotions, moods, perceptions and actions. According to research, people make a subconscious judgment about a product in fewer than 90 seconds, and a majority base that assessment on colour alone.[3]

> *'Testers for 7-Up consistently found consumers would report more lemon flavor in their product if they added 15% more yellow coloring to the package.'*

Malcolm Gladwell, *Blink: The Power of Thinking Without Thinking*

According to colorcom.com a black and white image holds the attention for 0.6 of a second, but a coloured image can hold the attention for two seconds or more (which is why we charged more for colour advertising sites when I worked in press).

---

2   Source www.cbsnews.com/news/texas-jail-is-small-but-in-the-pink
3   www.webfx.com

After the moody monochrome, greiges and beiges of the 1990s and early 2000s, (think Calvin Klein ads and Gwyneth Paltrow's wardrobe), I've noticed that colour has been steadily on the rise ever since. I believe that this is a reaction to the austere and unsure political and economic times we are currently living in (and if you're reading this in the future – does everyone use hoverboards to get to school yet?). Colour brings a breath of positive energy into our world.

Choosing the right brand colours

It's best practice for your designer to design your logo in black and white first and get the form and concept right, undistracted by colour. Your logo needs to work in monochrome (black, white or tints of black, called 'greyscale') if it is to be reproduced in photocopies, newspapers, merchandise or one-colour print jobs.

A lot of brands keep their logos black and white, especially product-based and luxury brands where gorgeous product photography adds the colour, e.g. Apple, Chanel, Mercedes Benz. Even brands like Adidas and John Lewis have taken this route.

However, if you have a service-based business and beautifully-designed items are not part of your offering, colour is key to bringing your brand to life.

Look back to your competitor analysis on your mood board. Do you see any colour trends or clichés for your industry? For example, a lot of technology companies are blue and organic ones are green and brown. If you want to stand out and subliminally communicate that you are different, colour is a great way to do so.

But don't just pick your favourite colours. A knowledge of colour psychology will add a whole other dimension to your brand, evoking the right emotions in your target customer.

What different colours mean

The human eye can detect seven million different colours,[4] and different combinations will change the context and meaning of the colours you select. But here's a list of some basic colours and what they represent.

- Dark blue: authoritative, reliable, established, masculine, corporate, ambitious, gravitas

- Mid-blue: communicative, open, trustworthy, caring, calm, secure, safe

- Paler blue: calm, idealistic, free, creative, inspiring

- Orange: positive, attention-grabbing, optimistic, hopeful, friendly, cheerful, change, exciting, energetic

- Turquoise: creative, calm, harmonious, spiritual

- Bright/light green: organic, fresh, healthy, growth, outdoorsy, relaxing

- Darker 'racing' green: heritage, high-end, class, luxury, old-money

- Yellow: happy, positive, warm, upbeat, illuminating, stimulating, energetic, encourages movement and communication, eye-catching

- Red: powerful, fast, youthful, bold, energetic, stimulating, attention-grabbing, love, passionate, dangerous, impulsive, intense

---

4   www.colormatters.com/color-and-vision/color-and-vision-matters

- Purple: creative, imaginative, royal, wealthy, empathic, wise, luxurious, quality

- Pink: feminine, gentle, soft, young, romantic (pastel), sexy (hot pink)

- Brown: organic, environmentally-aware, wholesome, old-fashioned, rugged, outdoorsy, natural

- Cream/beige: sophisticated, high-end, old-fashioned, traditional, retro

- Grey: balanced, calm, grounded, sophisticated, modern, neutral

- Black: luxurious, sophisticated, glamorous, strong, clear, simple, timeless, serious, formal, gravitas

- White (and white space): purity, innocence, luxury, calm, clean, peace

Of course, no colour will get the same reaction from everyone. We are all affected by our unique experiences. I had to wear a dark brown school uniform and the kids from other schools would shout out poo-related insults, so clearly now I would never entertain it for my own company branding. Colours also take on different nuances depending on the other colours combined with it, so cream with black might look modern and high-end, but with brown it looks more traditional or retro.

Different cultures may also have different meanings for colours - worth noting if you are going global. Red is the colour of luck, health, wealth and prosperity in Eastern cultures. White is traditionally worn by the bride in western cultures as a symbol of purity, but in Hinduism this absence of colour is worn in mourning – my maternal grandmother wore white for the rest of her life after my grandfather died.

How many colours should my branding have?

Most of the top brands – 95% – use only one or two colours for their logo. The most popular colours for logos are blue (33%), red (29%), black/silver/grey (28%) and yellow/gold (13%).

Of course, some global giants totally smash that rule, like Google, Microsoft and, previously, Apple. In the right hands, clearly rules can be broken, but if you are on a budget, fewer colours will look more high-end.

Even with a one-colour logo, a brand palette – a set of colours chosen for your brand identity – will give your branding more depth and variety. I normally look at three to five colours for a brand palette, usually one or two key colours (often including logo colour(s) and sometimes called primary colours, although not the red/blue/yellow meaning of primary we learned about at school), then another two or three secondary colours. You don't have to use all the colours all the time or on every page or item.

If you have a tonal brand palette where your colours are all different shades of one colour, consider a contrasting 'pop' colour like I did for Shifts to Success.

Here, a deep blue (authority, trust, reliability, gravitas) is the primary colour to resonate with the company's police officer audience. The secondary colours are a coordinating mid-blue (communication, ambition, caring, openness, trust), a paler blue (inspiration, freedom, big ideas, creativity) and a 'pop' colour of orange (positive, friendly, optimism, hope, change).

'Pop' colours bring life to a palette and are useful for drawing attention to important information, calls-to-action or buttons on a website.

Your designer will help you choose your brand palette but if you want more colour inspiration, Google 'colour wheel theory' and I highly recommend www.colourlovers.com or www.colordrop.io.

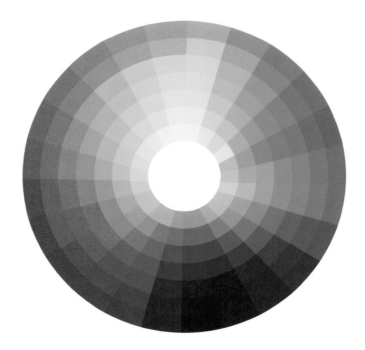

A colour wheel: Google or ask your designer about the theory but a quick tip is that your brand's 'pop' colours lie opposite your brand's main colours

Imagery

As they say, 'a picture paints a thousand words'. Strong imagery will lift your branding from blah to brilliant, build your brand with a distinctive look, and can help communicate a concept, emotion, story or idea better than words alone. Imagery includes:

- Photography
- Illustration
- Infographics, diagrams and tables
- Patterns, textures, shapes, symbols and icons

Photography

Great photography is the most powerful way to build your brand so we'll spend the most time on this one.

Stock photography: Great if you are tight on time and/or budget. I find Shutterstock excellent for the sheer variety and the affordable packages, but there are so many good, paid-for and free stock imagery websites out there now (just Google them). With the free images, do check the terms of usage – you may need to credit the photographer or site.

Warning: stock pictures often come with a side order of cheese. Try to avoid all the cringeworthy clichés – cheesy smiles, thumbs-ups, exaggerated worried faces, punching the air or high-fiving success. Basically anything a bit 'David Brent' in *The Office*. Other kinds of clichéd imagery to avoid include using metaphorical coastal scenery and sunrises, pictures of mountains

Stock photography has a dark side. Seriously, how exciting can a pie-chart be?!

and confusing sign-posts for any type of coaching. Most businesses are about helping people, so bring your brand promise to life with natural-looking (non-cheesy) images of your target customers looking happy and living the dream, presumably after they've bought your product or service.

Never just take an image from another website or Google image search – you will be infringing somebody's copyright. Besides, print images should be 300 dots per inch (DPI) and online they are usually only 72 DPI. Printing from low-resolution online images will mean blurry, pixelated results.

Note that if your designer buys your stock image for you, they own the licence for it, not you, unless they sign over the rights to you. If you own the licence, you can re-use the image on your social media, in blogs, etc. Better to purchase images yourself once your designer has helped you choose them.

Lorna Reeves, MyOhMy Weddings

Bespoke photography: Hiring your own professional photographer gives you the chance to tailor a set of unique images for your brand, and you can feature in them too. Do not DIY your brand shots with a phone; bad lighting or composition will just make your company look cheap and amateur. Great photography need not cost the earth and pro photographers can do miracles with post-production adjustments if necessary.

Ask for recommendations and check out photographers' websites. Photographers, like designers, tend to specialise. If you work in fitness and want fast-moving action shots, consider a sports photographer. If you put on events, see if you can get a wedding photographer (they might be cheaper in the week). If you work in nutrition, consider hiring a food photographer. They will think about things specific to your industry that more general photographers might not. Use your mood board to brief them on your brand and what you're looking to achieve.

If you want to use the images on your website, ask the photographer to shoot landscape format with a lot of 'background' left and right. This will allow the web developer to 'bleed' the image right to the edges of the screen if the layout requires this, and the focus of the image should still be visible when it crops on mobile.

Aim for ten to twelve usable brand images from the shoot with similar lighting and a tonal colour palette (try weaving your brand colours in) so your photography all looks like part of a set. Include pictures of you. People buy from people, so it's nice for potential customers to see your lovely face.

Keep your clothing simple, timeless and avoid anything too distinctive, distracting, trendy, fussy, patterned or with logos on. One client made the mistake of wearing a gorgeous patterned dress for her brand shoot, but then felt she couldn't wear it again in real life. Also avoid white shirts with black trousers or skirts, which cut you in half and can make you look like a waiter. Unless you work in hospitality and that's exactly the look you're going for. In which case, fill your boots!

Feature your brand colours in your outfits, surroundings and/or your props. Bring a couple of changes of outfits, tops, jackets or accessories for variety across the pictures. Refer back to 'Personal branding' in Part 1 if you need styling before the shoot.

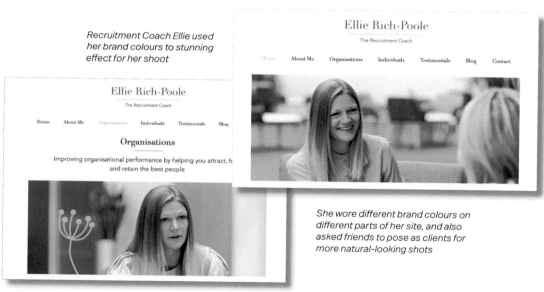

Recruitment Coach Ellie used her brand colours to stunning effect for her shoot

She wore different brand colours on different parts of her site, and also asked friends to pose as clients for more natural-looking shots

If your business demands client confidentiality but you want some pictures of you 'in action', ask two or three friends to pose as a 'client' with their backs to the camera whilst you are 'having a conversation' with them and facing the camera. Brief them on the dress and colour code too.

If you're a speaker and want more speaking gigs, book a photographer for your next event (or create an event).

Ask your photographer for landscape-format shots with plenty of background left and right for online usage, portrait-format shots and headshots. Use your new images with your brand colours and typefaces to give a coordinated look and feel across your printed and online media.

Headshots: Use one headshot consistently for your business profile pictures on social media, with your bio, for press releases, on your book jacket, etc. If your look has changed, make sure your profile pictures look up to date – you don't want to turn up anywhere and people not recognise you.

Look at the camera – eyes are important and invite the viewer in. Don't airbrush all your little creases out – that's character, experience and wisdom. I knew someone who tried airbrushing his imperfections out himself and ended up looking like Kryten (*Red Dwarf* fans can rejoice at the geeky reference).

Smile! It shows that you enjoy what you do. If you really don't like your teeth, make like the Mona Lisa, all enigmatic, or 'smize' like supermodel Tyra Banks (look it up, it's a thing).

Generally, colour headshots look friendlier and warmer than black and white. The only time I would 'go mono' is if I've got to unify several people's headshots when putting them together in a brochure or on a website.

Avoid a plain-background passport-style studio shoot. Tell a story. Make a statement. Stand out! Find an environment that suits you and your business. My personal brand pictures were taken against a graffitied wall to give a feeling of energy and raw creativity – much more dynamic than a studio shoot or me 'working at my computer' (yawn).

If you work with food, shoot in a kitchen, a farmer's market or an orchard. If you organise weddings, wear a 'smart guest' outfit and use a stunning hotel with beautiful grounds. If you work with children or animals... you're already ignoring that age-old advice, so give it a try (with parental/owner permission, of course). If you work outdoors or with natural products, use nature's beauty as your backdrop. Ask your photographer to shoot with a 'shallow depth of field' which will blur your background a bit and make sure you are the focus.

Colin Revie, Run the Day

Michael Coates, Combat Pest Control

A last note: if you are mixing photography from different sources, make sure the pictures go together stylistically for your new branding scheme with similar lighting, colours and settings. Your designer might be able to help by unifying them with filters, tints or pops of your brand colours, making them all black and white or overlaying graphics on top.

Illustration

Illustration is a great way to make your branding stand out and can add life and a unique character to your brand. Again, you can go for stock or bespoke illustrations and use them alongside or instead of photography.

Stock illustrations come as 'bitmap' or 'vector' images (see 'Jargon Buster'). Vector images are completely editable so your designer can use a section of the illustration, delete, duplicate, add to or scale elements and re-style it with your brand palette and fonts. Alternatively, they may be able to create bespoke illustrations for you or help you commission a professional illustrator.

Part of a set of illustrations created for Find Peace of Mind

Infographics, diagrams and tables

Great infographics, diagrams or tables make complex concepts simpler, more memorable and consolidate your thinking. Examples in this book would be the DoSaySee model and the VISION process diagram. Your designer might create these from scratch or start with a vector stock graphic, then redraw, scale, delete or add elements and customise it with your brand typefaces, colours, logo, etc.

Patterns, textures, shapes, symbols and icons

Patterns, textures, shapes, symbols and icons add richness, depth, variety and interest to your branding scheme. Shapes, symbols or icons will break copy up, emphasise areas or give dynamism and interest to a design and add a consistent style to your brand.

Spreads from a brochure for Specialist Retailers. Diagonals were a recurrent theme

Patterns and textures may take the form of repeat or irregular, e.g. geometric spots, stripes or shapes, or more organic, hand-drawn or painterly effects. Or they could be photographs, e.g. a close up of fabric texture, wallpaper, ripples on a pond, laser beams in the dark. If you're using any image as a background with text running over it, choose low contrast images or out the type in a tinted or opaque box to make sure you can still read it. (See examples in the Brochure section in the Output chapter.)

For all forms of imagery, the possibilities are literally endless, so add any appealing images to your mood board and look back at your FABs for inspiration. Talk with your designer to guide you through the right options to match your brand.

Case study: MyOhMy Weddings

Lorna Reeves is the founder of MyOhMy Weddings. Having already named the company and developed the strapline 'Your time to stand out and be proud', Lorna now wanted me to help her develop an aspirational, stylish brand for her affluent LGBTQ+ market.

Type: we avoided the swirly, girly script typefaces so often used by the wedding industry, and instead went for a more unisex, elegant and classic serif font. We also chose to set the name in title case, which was more gender-neutral than lower case (more feminine) or upper case (more masculine).

Colour: Lorna didn't want pink or rainbow LGBTQ+ clichés. Pinks are also popular in the wedding industry as they mainly focus on the bride, so this was another reason to avoid the colour. Instead, we paired a sophisticated rose gold with a unisex grey. The gradient effect added a shimmer, which Lorna felt made it look 'breathy, like a sigh'. Her business cards, printed with a special rose-gold metallic ink on one side, gave a truly luxurious feel.

Imagery: We found the wedding industry equally riddled with clichés: flowers, rings, hearts and, of course, heterosexual brides and grooms. So how to stand out? It was only when we started exploring the much wider concept of love that we struck gold. For those in the LGBTQ+ community who still have to fight for equality, the image of the dove symbolises love, peace, hope and the freedom to marry who they want, where and how they want to.

Lorna actually cried when she finally saw her vision come to life, via this powerful combination of type, colour and imagery.

MyOhMy Weddings, from top, L-R:
logo, cards printed in a rose gold
metallic ink, dove and imagery

Output

'Everybody that's successful lays a blueprint out.'

Kevin Hart, comedian, actor, producer

The output section of the VISION process is the summation of everything we have worked on so far, pulling it all together into your brand guidelines. I have included brochures and websites in this chapter too, as typically my clients get these designed as soon as they've got their brand guidelines.

Brand guidelines

If strategy is to design what foundations are to a mansion, then brand guidelines are the blueprints. When you apply them consistently across everything: - your business cards to your social media, brochure, website and even your business premises – you create a strong look and feel that customers can easily recognise and identify within seconds.

A branding project should culminate in a set of guidelines for your shiny new brand. Brand guidelines are a business asset and add value to your company when it comes to seeking investment or exiting. They protect your brand, so they protect your company.

Your guidelines help keep your brand looking professional and coordinated. Consistent visual output helps your audience easily identify your company, wherever you show up.

Brand guidelines are usually provided as a PDF so you can send them to anyone producing your assets – staff, graphic designers, video producers, marketing agencies, photographers, social media managers, partnership companies, book publishers or web developers. They prevent the need for lots of trial and error, saving everyone time and you money.

What should your brand guidelines include?

Typical brand guidelines explain the purpose, significance and usage of your brand to help any supplier understand what your company is all about and produce assets to help build your brand. They should include everything you've worked through in the VISION process (other agencies may call these elements by different names – 'Inner Brand' especially is a phrase I coined – but the principles are the same):

- Brand vision (or what some call a mission statement)
- Inner Brand: brand values, personality, voice
- Logo variations and usage guidelines

- Typefaces: the logo fonts and typefaces for professional and internal usage:

  - Font guidelines for heading, body copy, captions, bullets and any other key uses, e.g. signage.

  - Website fonts: sources from where they may be purchased or free-to-use Google fonts if a match exists.

  - Microsoft Office fonts: for everyday word-processing, emails and PowerPoints, include a Microsoft Office typeface or two that complements your branding scheme. Your team can then create documents which still look 'on brand' and don't mess up when sent externally.

- Colour specifications for print and online media (RGB, CMYK, Pantone and HEX or HTML – all these are explained in Part 3)

- Photography guidelines: for purchasing stock images, briefing photographers and any stylistic effects (tints, filters, etc)

- Guidelines on any other illustrations, patterns, shapes, icons or infographics

Your brand guidelines can't be *too* prescriptive, as it's impossible to account for every eventuality when they are first developed. Also, different creatives will interpret the guidelines in their own way and that can keep things fresh and exciting over time (this only works if your designers are any good – I've seen some abominations produced in the wrong hands). Your guidelines should evolve as your company does, but do make sure suppliers read, understand and follow them in order to establish your brand when it launches.

Branding pack

My company provides a set of files with the guidelines at the end of each branding project. Our basic branding packages include:

- Logo files in different colourways and formats for print and online, with and without strapline (or so strapline can be cropped out)

  - Colour version

  - Black version (also called 'mono'; can be used for one-colour print jobs)

  - White version (also called 'reversed out')

- Social media icon: sits in as your 'profile picture' when you set up your business social pages. Needs to work at a tiny size on phone screens.

- Business card print-ready artwork.

- One-page brand guidelines

These elements allow you to show up in person or online looking 'branded', and allow you to brief other suppliers, so I would say this is the minimum to expect in a branding package. More in-depth branding projects may include elements like pattern, colour, shapes, icons, photography briefs, stock images and guidelines, infographics, etc.

Recommended file formats

These file formats are pretty universal, so you should have your logos supplied in all of them. There is more information on these in Part 3.

JPEG: for digital. Use these for your email sign off, in social media, blogs and internally-produced documents. JPEGs have opaque backgrounds and are bitmap images so will blur if you scale them up.

PNG: for your web developer and other digital usage. I supply these logos with transparent backgrounds so developers can use them over an image or coloured panel.

EPS: for print and animation. These files are so useful for your graphic designer, publisher, animator, videographer, and they work in your internal documents like PowerPoints. The vector format scales with no loss of clarity. Supplied with transparent backgrounds, developers can then overlay them on an image or coloured panel. Ask your designer to convert EPS 'text to outlines'. This makes the wording in the logo non-editable but stable, so it doesn't matter if people don't have your logo fonts on their system.

AI: the raw Adobe Illustrator file, editable for future changes.

PDF: your reference file.

A couple of other formats:

Spot-colour EPS: only needed if you wish to print a logo on merchandise in more than one colour. For one-colour logos, just use the black logo provided and specify any colour.

SVG: online vector files that scale like EPS files.

Brochures

A core part of building your brand, a brochure will make you seem more polished in meetings, is an impressive leave-behind and makes everything more tangible to your prospective clients. Prospects are also less likely to haggle if your prices are printed on an 'official' document.

So how do you create a stand out brochure? Firstly, establish its purpose to focus the content. What do you want people to do? Keep the end game in mind as you write your copy.

How long should your brochure be? As a rule of thumb, 1,000–1,500 words is plenty, which will create an eight to twelve page A4 brochure. See 'Brand voice' in the Inner Brand chapter for tips on writing copy.

My team and I use this as a basis for our clients' brochure content:

- Introduction (write briefly about you, what you do, perhaps your story).

- An outline of your client and their problems (so readers can quickly tell you understand them).

- How you can help them (your service/products/method. What makes you different? Paint a picture of their life transformed after working with you).

- Testimonial(s) – social proof from clients is powerful.

- What you are selling – packages? A bespoke solution?

- Next steps – a call-to-action (CTA), e.g. register, contact, offer, apply or buy.

Brochure format

Consider the shape, size and usage of your brochure. If you're going to mail it, stick to sizes you can fit in an envelope. If your brochures are to go in gift/event bags, if you are in a creative industry or want to stand out, then you could have a landscape, square or bespoke 'die-cut' format, a mini-brochure or one that folds out into a poster. Not all unusual formats cost more. Google image search 'brochure formats', save a few interesting ideas to your mood board and talk them over with your designer.

Most brochures are created with folded pieces of paper. One folded piece of A3 will create four A4 pages (front cover, back cover and two pages in the middle spread), so you can't add one, two or three pages if you decide to add some extra information – it always has to be four. You can have a one or two-page flyer, but that's just a piece of paper printed on one or two sides. After that, it's four, eight, twelve, sixteen, etc pages.

Remember that a leaflet on a thinner stock will feel more disposable and less impressive than a brochure with a heavier weight stock and a laminated cover. Read the chapters on paper specifications and special finishes in Part 3 and speak to your designer about who you are targeting and what you are trying to achieve.

Lastly, as well as a print version of your brochure always ask for a PDF version that you can attach to an email or people can download.

Layout tips

Rather than looking at your own industry publications, look at beautiful magazines for inspiration and a more aspirational look.

White space: Essential to good design (although not always actually white), 'white space' is just a designer term for space in layouts. White space conveys sophistication, calm, modernity, luxury, cleanliness and simplicity. It allows the reader to breathe, pause, reflect on and easily navigate a design. Don't cram too much in as if trying to get your money's worth out of every inch of paper. Too much information is overwhelming; white space helps the eye focus on what is important. Use big margins, white space and beautiful images; up your number of pages, drop your word count. White space takes your brand from economy to first class...

Take your brand from economy to first class with white space...

Imagery will break up copy, help tell your story, add visual interest and simplify difficult concepts. See 'Imagery' in the previous chapter for more information. Use your brand colours as well to segment information and ease navigation.

Typography: You're not the designer, so I'm leaving most of the heavy-lifting to them, but here are a few basic legibility tips to keep an eye out for:

- Your optimum line length is approximately ten to twelve words. Much longer line lengths mean the reader might have to re-read them; shorter ones feel a bit stop-start and slow readers down again.

- 8–12 pt is a good copy size. I tend to err on the larger side (10–12 pt) as we have an ageing population. Small print and captions can go in 6–8 pt. Size headings up for visual interest; I like to go at least twice the size of the body copy, if not three times or more.

- Avoid widows and orphans. Ban them by editing your copy, adjusting previous word breaks, using deliberate hyphenations or a change in line 'tracking' (ask your designer).

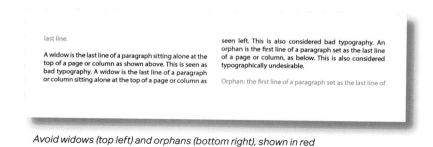

Avoid widows (top left) and orphans (bottom right), shown in red

- Where possible, avoid splitting brand, people or product names and awkward word-breaks over two lines.

- Up to 8% of men (4.5% of the population) are colour-blind, so make sure type is well contrasted (light/dark) against its background, regardless of colour. Photocopy the design if you're unsure or turn it black and white digitally.

Beware of reduced type legibility when combining type with colours and images

- With text over an image, a high contrast image will make text illegible. High contrast for text, low contrast for images is best. Use a tinted box to knock back the image contrast or have the whole photo made lighter or darker to reduce the contrast in the image and increase contrast for the text.

Proofing. Ask your designer or printer to get a digital proof of your brochure made up, using the correct paper stock (if possible), before you go to print, so you can:

- Check the colours (note, all proofs are an indication only).

- See how the copy looks. Too big or small in real life?
  Not legible enough?

- Pick up on typos or mistakes you may have missed on screen.

- Get a 'feel' for the finished brochure. Is the stock too thin or thick?

You cannot preview proofs for most special print finishes (see Chapter 14) so you will have to view previous printer/designer examples to get an idea of how they might look.

Grid structures. A grid is like an invisible 'skeleton' that your brochure elements hang off. That means the margins are the same on all the pages, column widths are consistent and all text and pictures are aligned to this 'grid'.

You can have a one, two or three, or even four column grid structure. Of course, your designer can artfully place elements 'breaking out' of the grid for impact, but a consistent structure to the layout helps the reader navigate the document.

Google different magazine or brochure grid layouts, save the ones you like and discuss them with your designer.

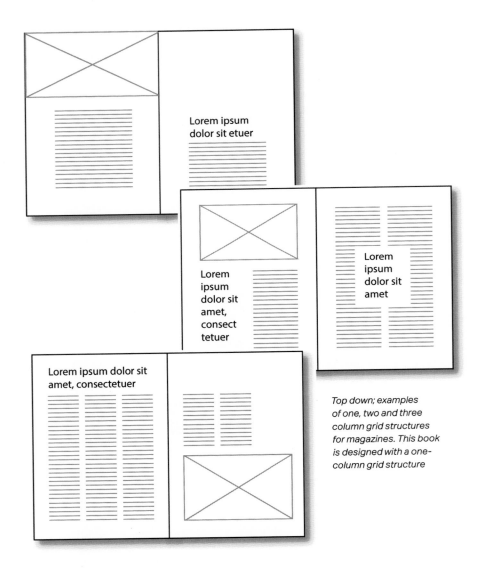

Lorem ipsum
dolor sit etuer

Lorem
ipsum
dolor sit
amet,
consect
tetuer

Lorem
ipsum
dolor sit
amet

Lorem ipsum dolor sit
amet, consectetuer

*Top down; examples
of one, two and three
column grid structures
for magazines. This book
is designed with a one-
column grid structure*

Lastly, a couple of brochure tips that have nothing to do with branding but are good to know:

- A form on a brochure makes it subject to value added tax (VAT) because it becomes a sales tool. However, brochures are VAT-exempt if there's no form as they are classed as 'books and other printed literature'. Print sales forms separately so you will just be charged VAT on those. If you are VAT registered, you can ignore this tip.

- Keep print runs small so that, as your company inevitably evolves and changes, you won't be left with too many out-of-date brochures to recycle..

Websites

The digital age has meant that geography is no longer an issue, so there is no reason why your brand can't reach an international audience. My company works with developer partner agencies, but we often get involved with the design, planning the UX (how people navigate the site), information hierarchy (what info sits where), copy-writing/editing and project management.

Designing and building a website are usually two different disciplines. Developers tend to specialise in either the front-end (the look and UX) or back-end (functionality). It's rare, in my experience, to find developers that do both really well, although you should find both skillsets in a good web agency. Even if you're building your own site though, some of these tips will still be of use.

As with brochures, you need to first work out the purpose of your website. Is it a 'brochure site' showcasing your business or does it need to do more?

Generally speaking, take your brochure copy and halve the content again (at least). At the moment, nearly half of all website traffic worldwide is via mobile.[1] That's a tiny area to make a big impact. Less is best. Short blocks of text and bullet points are helpful.

Structure

Standard brochure site content might be arranged like this:

- Homepage – setting the tone. Headline message or video to grab the attention.

- About us – usually about the company, an overview of what you do and why.

- Clients/case studies – showing you understand clients' problems, showcasing your solutions and testimonials. These may be on dedicated client pages or dotted throughout the site.

- Products/services – may or may not have prices on.

- Team – introduce yourself and your team members. Customers like to see who they are dealing with.

- Blog – changing your website content regularly helps it to get found by search engines.

- Contact us - only ask for the info you need and make sure you are GDPR (General Data Protection Regulation) compliant.

---

1 www.statista.com/statistics/277125/share-of-website-traffic-coming-from-mobile-devices

Additional functionality may include:

- Quiz or scorecard for lead generation
- Sign-up pages for webinars or other content, e.g. downloadable PDFs, white papers, menus, e-books or brochures
- Splash pages
- Data collection and integration into a content management system
- Online booking system, e.g. for tables in a restaurant or consultation slots
- Membership areas of the site, e.g. online learning portal
- Donation or subscription pages
- Search functionality
- Pop-ups
- Chat boxes
- E-commerce
- Video

Information hierarchy

Your information hierarchy is basically just organising the information that should appear on your website. You need a heading for each section of information ('About', 'Contact', etc) and then an idea of what appears under each header. Map it out with sticky notes or sketch it out like a flow chart.

My team and I simplified the Centenary Lounge website from twenty to thirty pages to just seven main headings.

Home page > images/video, headline copy, scrolling banner leading to other parts of the site.

Navigation across the top:

- Book button > choose Birmingham or Worcester > booking form

- Our story > history, about the founder, awards, etc

- Locations > Worcester, Birmingham Moor St, Birmingham Snow Hill overview > three individual location pages, each with a menu and contact details

- Occasions > events form > submit button

- Shop > overview information > 'Shop Now' button > items listings > add to basket > proceed to checkout

- News > blog stories

- Contact > bookings and general enquiries form > submit button

Wireframes and user experience (UX)

Once you have your information hierarchy, ask your web designer to map out a 'wireframe' so you can see the UX on each page: what information is found where; what users click or fill in where; how they navigate through the site and get back to the homepage.

Wireframes help you plan out what goes where on each page of your website and how the user will navigate through the site

You can sketch out your own wireframe to brief the web designer or ask them to produce one for you. This may be hand or computer-drawn as shown here

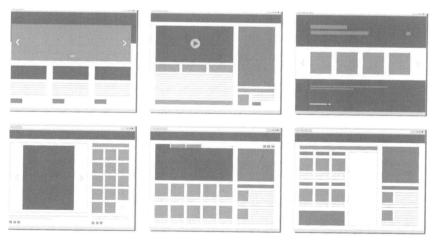

Wireframes can be hand- or computer-drawn with blank boxes to denote the pictures, but I sometimes add an indication of key imagery and colours too. The copy is usually indicated with 'lorem ipsum' or parallel lines.

Google 'Wireframes' to see how they are put together. Keep functionality vital and simple – the fewer clicks a user needs to complete a task or find information, the better. Look at your key competitors – and look at their information hierarchy to see what works and what doesn't. Is the information easy to find?

Layout tips

Colour: Use one colour from your brand palette (your 'pop' colour if you have one) to denote where visitors can click to find out more, watch a video, sign up or submit information. A consistent colour and shape of button 'trains' the visitor to take action when you need them to.

White space: My constant request to web developers is, 'Can you put more white space in?' Don't cram the copy tightly; give it room to breathe. As with brochures, keep a clean layout with lots of white space, big margins and great imagery to make your site easy on the eyes. Check your FABs or competitors for inspiration.

Images. Check the previous section on Imagery for general guidelines. Choose landscape-format images with a lot of background left and right and a central focus if you want a picture to go right across your web page on desktop and still work when it crops on mobile. Always download your images at the highest resolution (for print usage) and ask your developer to copy and optimise them for web (i.e. shrink the file size, so your website loads quickly). Web-optimised images cannot be used for print so be sure to keep the high-resolution images too.

Social media specifications

I always get asked, 'What size should the profile pictures, timeline images, posts and ads be for each platform?' Facebook, Twitter, LinkedIn, Instagram and so on can all change their specs, layouts and functionality at any time, and new social media platforms may launch, so any information I give you here may date quickly. The best thing to do is to Google the relevant platforms or ask your social media specialist.

In this chapter, we have looked at the results of your branding project, starting with your brand guidelines and brand pack. We looked at brochures and websites as these are the main brand assets people tend to get developed once they have their new brand guidelines.

Your brand guidelines should be used for every aspect of your branding, so speak to your designer about what outputs you need to grow your business and make sure you use them to stay coordinated and on brand as you grow.

Nurture

'A great brand is a story that is never completely told.'

Scott Bedbury, branding consultant

By working through the VISION process, you should now have all the building blocks you need to look great, stand out in your industry and communicate with clarity. But only if you use your new assets *consistently* can you build brand recognition and familiarity to help you grow your business. The challenge is maintaining your brand identity as you generate more content and an increasing amount of people start producing assets for you.

The Nurture stage looks at what happens once your branding project is complete, you've paid your brand designer and you're left alone with your new baby. You cannot neglect your brand or branding and expect them to flourish. You need to nurture and look after them to help them grow and evolve.

Nurturing your brand

Once a shiny new brand is released into the world, even with the most thorough of brand guidelines, clients and their suppliers still manage to (mis)interpret them in a way the brand designer may never have imagined possible, ignore them completely or feel compelled to put their own 'creative spin' on things. In the hands of a great designer, this can add depth and richness to the branding solution, but more often, my clients come back to me and ask, '*Were they* meant *to do that?*'

Simply owning brand guidelines does not guarantee immunity against design disasters.

Your beautiful brand in the hands of the enthusiastic and uninitiated can quickly unravel and look unkempt, messy and inconsistent. As with business coaching, personal training or any other type of service where benefits are cumulative over time, you will only see the ROI if everyone sticks to the plan. Read your brand guidelines and *make sure they are applied* or you will lose the very style, consistency and recognition you've just paid good money for.

And if you are the boss, don't start messing and 'getting creative' with the identity yourself. You'll be giving a clear message to your team that they can do the same. It's like the 'broken window' phenomenon that former New York mayor Rudy Giuliani made famous. Your brand is eroded by an unnecessary bit of creative licence here, an additional colour or typeface there, and before you know it, all branding hell breaks loose and the brand becomes unrecognisable again.

In *The Creative Curve* by Allen Gannett, he writes about research from the University of Michigan which indicates that the more familiar we are with something, the more we like it and have positive associations with it.

People want their brands to be consistent. You will never see Ford, Virgin or McDonald's switching up their colours or fonts too suddenly (and customers get upset when well-loved brands do this). But we also have a craving for novelty. The same research shows that people start to tire of seeing the same thing after eight times.

That's why you and your team may want to get creative with your new brand, but resist the urge, because the point at which you may be getting bored could be when your customers are just starting to recognise your company. According to brand expert Pam Moore, it takes five to seven exposures before a person starts to recognise your brand – let alone take action.

Consistency is the key to relationship-building, familiarity, recognition, confidence and trust. Remember you are marketing human-to-human, not B2B or B2C. People relate to brands in a similar way as they do to people, so build the relationship by showing up consistently and reliably.

Imagine you made a new friend who was sophisticated with short blonde hair. Then the next time you met up, they had spiky blue hair, a pierced nose and leathers. Next time, flowing locks and tie-dyed garments. You wouldn't recognise them each time they showed up, would be confused about who they were or what they stood for, and would likely find it difficult to make a strong connection with them. It's no different with your brand.

I cannot make this point enough, so I'll say it three times.

Consistency is key. Consistency is key. Consistency is key.

Please, just stick to your guidelines. In the first three months at least, I recommend asking your brand designer or agency to help you, your team and your suppliers get trained up to roll out your new brand. It's like a recipe for a dish in a Michelin-starred restaurant – in the right hands, that recipe will yield an award-winning result, but without the right knowledge and skills, things can quickly go wrong. The head chef needs to train the team to make sure standards are maintained by every single person. Maintaining standards and consistency is key to Michelin-level success, which is why I developed the Nurture part of the VISION process – it picks up where most branding projects end. This stage helps your brand get established, take root and flourish beautifully.

Evolving your brand

Your team is trained up, everything looks great and your rebrand is working for you. Hurray! You can put your feet up and relax now, right?

Ah no, sorry. Like your company, your brand is a living, breathing entity and is never 'done' or complete. Keeping your branding static and unchanged for too long will send a message out that your business hasn't changed. Stay aware of what's going on around you in terms of technology and styling and if your company changes, it's prudent to run a quick healthcheck on whether your branding is still relevant for you.[1] I advise my clients to steer clear of 'trendy' designs to give their new branding longevity, but for start-ups, I look at three to five years for the average lifespan of a brand identity. Most start-ups change so much in the first five years and the business landscape is ever-changing, so their identities will likely need to be tweaked to keep up as their company focus, offering, niche or the market changes. A more established company may plan for its branding having a shelf-life of five to ten years, with ongoing nips and tucks to keep it looking fresh.

---

1   www.InnerVisions-ID.com/quiz

Clearly, whilst consistency is key, it's also important to evolve subtly and strategically. This is where a long-term relationship with your designer or agency will help you grow, nurture and evolve the brand over time and with control.

What if my business or focus changes?

Once you have built a level of brand equity and recognition, evolution not revolution is the way forward. For example, you may redesign your website and brochures, tweak the logo, change the strapline.

Evolving your brand is an extended version of the nurture process over time. To use a plant analogy, you prune your brand by culling outdated parts, and feed and water it by reinvesting in it to keep it vital, alive and growing.

One thing I would really warn against is changing things just for the sake of it or because you are bored. It is best to make any changes to your brand to align with changes in the business. If there is no justifiable reason to change, proceed with caution, or at least, don't do anything major. Even iconic brands have to keep tweaking their branding to keep things fresh, but the best evolutions have a strategy behind them and align with what the times and the customer needs.

A great example is Coca Cola. Coke Classic was always in a red can and the sugar-free Coke Zero in a black can with a flash of red. In 2016, Coke pulled its cans into line by making them all red with just a different colour band at the top to differentiate their variants. With sugar taxation and a general move towards a healthier lifestyle, the idea was to make Coke Zero more appealing to regular, or lapsed, Coke Classic drinkers.

In 2010, Gap spent an estimated $100 million on a global rebrand that was universally slated and rejected by brand fans and the design industry alike.

Gap's United States CEO then angered the design community by asking them to submit ideas for free to replace the new logo, showing a clear disregard for any brand strategy, equity, heritage, or their time and expertise. Gap reinstated its old logo a few days later, so if you blinked, you likely missed it. Four months later, the CEO left the company.[2]

I think the problem with the Gap rebrand was that there was no clear strategy or reason for change as the business itself hadn't changed at all. Fancying a change is not a good reason for a rebrand. Consumers like familiarity in their brands (especially for a brand like Gap, where consistency is part

---

2   www.theguardian.com/media/2010/oct/12/gap-logo-redesign

of the appeal – my husband buys his Gap jeans in minutes without trying them on because he knows the style doesn't change).

Weight Watchers also rebranded to WW.com at the end of 2018, evolving its messaging towards 'wellness that works'. The brand instantly went from a well-known name with a strong promise to one that people no longer recognised nor understood. This reportedly wiped 34% off Weight Watchers' share price almost overnight.[3]

If nothing has changed about your business and things are going well, don't switch things up without good reason. But as your company develops, your brand should reflect this – the key is to introduce changes with caution and control.

Times when you might need a rebrand or a brand extension include when you are:

- **Targeting a new or different demographic.** You may wish to provide new goods or services and not dilute your original offering, e.g. Armani has Giorgio, Emporio, Privé, Collezioni, Jeans, Junior and Exchange brand extensions for different markets.

- **Changing focus or direction.** An Australian company, Web Traffic That Works, was niching to focus on raising its clients' profiles on LinkedIn, so we rebranded them to Prominence Global.

- **Expanding into new territories.** You may need a name change to unify a global marketing strategy, e.g. the UK's Marathon bars rebranded to Snickers for the worldwide audience.

---

3   www.impactbnd.com/blog/what-marketers-can-learn-from-wws-rebrand-troubles

- **Entering into mergers or acquisitions.** The merger of Orange and T-Mobile created EE in 2010, which was then bought out by BT.

- **Changing hands.** A new brand guardian in the business may wish to signal new beginnings, a change in strategy or focus.

- **Moving with the times.** Mastercard simplified its double roundel logo and dropped the name (so high was its brand recognition) so it would work better on digital platforms.

- **Differentiation.** To avoiding looking like your competition.

If you are going through any kind of rebrand, redo the branding assessment and go through the VISION process again to make sure you keep everything aligned to your evolving brand aspirations and business goals.

Protecting your brand

This is not strictly part of the VISION process, but it felt right to talk about protecting your intellectual property (IP) in the 'Nurture' part of this book. Protecting IP is something to consider when building your brand. Look at all aspects of your branding development with your IP in mind, from naming the company to creating your brand assets.

What constitutes IP?

IP is a 'unique creation of the human intellect'. You need to protect this as your company grows and attracts the attention of your competition. Imitation may be the sincerest form of flattery, but in business it can quickly do untold damage to that which you may have spent years creating. So what can – and can't – you protect?

An idea alone is not IP. For example, my idea for this book didn't count as my IP, but the words I have written are. IP protection incorporates copyright, trademarks, patents and designs (registered and unregistered). You get some types of protection automatically, others you have to apply for.

If you plan to scale or exit your company, your brand almost certainly will become a part of the negotiation, so you having ownership of your IP and brand assets is a definite bonus.

Having the right type of IP protection helps you to protect the names of your products or brands, your inventions, the design or look of your products or brand assets, the things you write, make or produce. For © copyright you will need to show that the other side copied your work. You don't need to show that for trademarks and patents, so a brand name that you came up with completely by yourself could easily still be trade mark infringement.

For absence of doubt, when I talk about 'design' in this book, I mean in a branding capacity, not the design of products. If designing a logo, say, in the absence of any suitable contract, there are statutory provisions (in the UK at least) to say that the author rather than the commissioner owns the copyright. This means your designer or the agency are likely to automatically own the copyright to your commissioned design.

Additionally, if the agency contracts freelancers on projects (whether you are aware of that arrangement or not), unless the agency has put their own agreement in place, the freelancer owns the copyright and not the agency.

This is because copyright isn't something anyone applies for – it automatically applies to the creator of any artistic asset (art, design, music, writing…). The idea behind modern copyright law is that if creatives can control who is allowed to copy their work, then they can charge for that permission. Copyright simply means that no one can replicate a creation without the owner's permission and different works are protected for different lengths of time.

Assuming your creative is not your employee and you don't already have contractual guidelines in place, if you are commissioning new work ask your creative to grant you the copyright of anything they produce for you and get that in writing before you engage their services. Day-to-day, owning the copyright matters because without a contractual agreement, if you wish to get your assets tweaked by another creative in the future, it is at the original creative's discretion and goodwill (as 'author' of the copyright) as to whether they will hand those files over to you or not. If they hold the copyright they could also resell that work. Some creatives may charge a fee for giving up their original files and/or transferring copyright over to you.

To put my clients' minds at ease, my agency's contracts and fees sign over copyright of all final approved and paid-for artwork, along with a copy of the editable files. I retain the right to use my team's work for publicity and advertising purposes, with client approval (and my clients tend to be proud that my company is showcasing their brand as an example of what we do).

Trade marks ™ and registered trade marks ® are super-important for a business to scale as they are used to identify unique assets pertaining to a business. This can include brand, company or product names, logos and other designs like infographics and symbols, straplines, tag-lines, slogans, or any combination of the above that identify a legal entity. Trade marks usually last for ten years before they need renewing. It is advisable to trade mark your brand name and logo, especially if you plan to scale or exit.

Your trade mark needs to be distinctive and unique and you also need to be careful of infringing someone else's trade mark. No one wants to launch their brand and then be sued for trade mark infringement. Generally speaking, the more indistinct the element, the harder it is to trade mark. If you have a name, logo, strapline and graphic device, say, the combination of all three will be the easiest to protect, but it is good to break down each of these and protect the elements too if possible as if you protect each item individually, you could potentially sue if someone used only one.

Patents protect physical and virtual inventions (including software) and advances in technology, but now we are completely outside the remit of this book, so I'll stop there, except to say that the laws and processes around copyright, trade mark and patents, are all different and the issue is hugely complex. These laws also vary across different countries, are liable to change and that you usually need to apply for every country you want protection in.

Using other people's creations

If you want to use other people's content (images, copy or music), you have to understand permissions and licensing, what is allowed and what isn't – it's a minefield. Your Facebook ad or YouTube video can get pulled immediately if it is set to music that you haven't paid the licence for and the owner of that music objects. There are music libraries that will provide you with cheap or free tunes. If you're hiring a professional film or video producer, they will be able to navigate these waters for you.

A common practice for many entrepreneurs is to illustrate blog posts with images found on the internet. If you are using an image without asking the image owner, then you are infringing their copyright. You may be allowed to 'borrow' it if you get permission from them, quote a source and/or give credit, making clear this is not your work or ownership. But there are so many free and affordable stock image sites these days, that's probably the easier option and the licensing terms will be detailed on there.

Big fat caveat: I am not a legal advisor and this chapter is only here to raise your awareness of general issues surrounding IP. For specific and up-to-date advice always speak to an IP law specialist and in the UK check the UK.Gov site on Intellectual Property for more information.

Part 2 summary

That brings us to the end of the VISION process. In working through it, you should now have the foundations to build a really solid company brand.

Visualise focused on your aspirations and vision for your brand and your company. We also, crucially, looked at your customers' vision and what their aspirations are.

Inner Brand developed the heart and soul, the emotive part of your brand values: a brand personality and a brand voice to build connection, trust, fans and loyalty from your customers.

Stand Out demonstrated three ways of making an impact and standing out from the competition: your company name, strapline, and knowing your competition and your industry landscape.

Image looked at the three visual elements of building your brand and the psychology of type, colour and imagery.

Output focused on the results of your branding project, brand guidelines, branding packs and gave you tips for developing brochures and websites.

Nurture looked at what happens after the branding process – rolling out your brand, how to manage your brand as your company evolves and how to protect your brand.

Following the VISION process will give you a brand that truly supports your business goals and ambitions. In the third section of the book, we will tackle the techy stuff and give you knowledge to help you turn all this theory into reality.

Part 3
The Techy Stuff

This part gets a bit technical, so you may need a cup of tea and a few biscuits to fortify you, but by the end, you'll be fully briefed in how to go about getting the brand of your dreams – and know how to articulate what you need and want.

Part 3 will tell you all about:

- Finding the right designer
- Colour specifications and print techniques
- Paper specifications
- Special finishes and binding

and finishes with a

- Jargon Buster

which will make you look really switched on to your designer, developer or printer. One of my clients said having the right information really helped him because his developers looked at him with 'a different filter' and gave him more respect once he could talk to them in their language. In his words:

'Instead of the monkeys, I was suddenly dealing with the organ grinder!'

Find the right designer to help grow your business

Find The Right Designer

'If you think good design is expensive, you should look at the cost of bad design.'

Dr Ralf Speth, automotive executive

Investing as much as you can on quality branding will pay for itself in the confidence it gives you and your clients. If you haven't found your brand designer yet, this chapter will give you a few pointers.

Design isn't one-size-fits-all; most designers have a specialism. No one can be great at everything, and although many graphic designers and even web designers say they provide branding services, in my experience, they often just mean logo design.

It makes sense that the best results will come from using specialists for each aspect of a project: branding consultants, graphic designers, web developers, photographers, illustrators, animators, videographers, packaging designers, etc. My company specialises in branding, but we may team up with another company for a packaging project. We can sort the branding, but our partner company will have the structural and materials know-how. We have a partnership network of web developers, illustrators, photographers – with project managers to oversee the whole thing and make sure objectives are met.

Where and how to find your designer

The reason it's hard to find a good designer is that the barrier to entry is so low. The price of technology is falling, the cost of higher-education rising, and fewer wannabe designers are bothering with qualifications. There are adverts on the London Underground promising a career as a graphic designer in just twelve weeks, but that will just be about learning which buttons to push.

I don't believe you can teach analytical and critical thinking, drawing, creative skills, design history, theory and strategy in that timeframe – all things that add meaning and depth to a design solution. Excellence is achieved through years of learning, experience, dedication and best practice. I've met some OK self-taught designers, but standards vary wildly, and in my experience, those who have studied design to any extent are easier to work with.

Wherever you're looking for your designer, check ratings and reviews, but also ask your potential hires to provide three references (and contact at least one). You should be looking for a partnership to help you develop your brand as your business grows.

Cheap-as-chips sites

I'm talking about the likes of Fiverr, Upwork, Freelancer.com. If you are a cash-strapped entrepreneur with more time than money, then these sites can be an accessible solution to give you a serviceable starter logo for less than the price of this book. You pay the site, and the site holds payment from the designer until you are happy with the job.

At this price point – low cost and fast-turnaround – no designer can take the time to truly understand your business and ambitions, so you risk ending up with a logo that does you more harm than good. People will be too polite to tell you your branding sucks, but quietly, almost imperceptibly, you'll be losing business.

Beware any designer who offers 'unlimited revisions'. They are guessing and throwing every kind of mud at the wall to see what sticks. They'll send you thirty logos to choose from, and if you don't like them, they'll churn out another thirty. This scattergun approach will eat up your time and sanity, and you're likely still to end up with something generic that you don't love, but it 'will do'. Yes, I know – give an infinite number of monkeys a Mac and one of them *may* come up with the Nike swoosh, but who's got the time to deal with monkeys?

If you're paying Primark prices, don't expect the results to be any more exclusive than one of its T-shirts. I discovered in a client's competitor analysis that he had an almost identical logo to someone else in the same field. He told me he knew about it because she had contacted him years before, saying that he was using *her* logo. Turns out they had both used the same cheap site, so they realised there was no point pursuing the matter further. Instead, they decided to carry on with their lookalike logos in their respective localities.

Even if you have no plans to go global, if another company is trademarking *its* logo, it can clamp down on your usage of any brand assets that look similar. My client was lucky this time, but when he was ready to scale, he decided to invest in a unique brand – something he could trademark and protect.

Portfolio sites

Bēhance, Dribbble – these sites showcase various designers' work and you contact the designers directly. The standard of design work does seem a lot higher, but you negotiate your own terms with the designer directly and the site won't protect you financially like the freelance sites do.

Word-of-mouth recommendations

This is always the best option: ask your networks. Pretty much all my clients find me this way. With technology, you don't even need to be in the same city or country to work together – I have clients in Europe, the United States and Australia as well as all over the UK.

Here are a few more tips that may help you avoid the crimes against design my clients have experienced in the past.

Does the designer 'get' you?

- Do you like their work? Do you feel listened to? Do you get on?
- Do you feel in safe hands? Can they clearly explain their process to you?
- Do they understand your specific challenges as an entrepreneur?
- Do they ask intelligent, thought-provoking questions? Do they seek to understand your business, your ambitions, your clients?

One of my clients spoke to a designer, and after a five-minute phone call, got sent three logo ideas. The results, unsurprisingly, were generic and totally wrong for what she was trying to achieve.

Any potential partner should take the time to get to know you and show an interest in what you do. I'm always shocked by how many don't.

Think bigger picture.

A branding partnership must include the capacity and expertise to grow with your business needs and help you strategically.

I had a client who'd previously gone to one designer for their logo, another for their training materials, another for their website and another for their book. You may, of course, use different specialists for different tasks, but if you don't have an overarching brand strategy and those important brand guidelines in place, you'll end up with a mess and nothing joined up.

Do they know their stuff?

Ask the designer how they will supply the files and how they produce their work. Avoid designers who create logos in Adobe Photoshop or brochures in Adobe Illustrator. (Other programmes exist, but Adobe is the industry standard). A Photoshop logo will not scale up without loss of quality, and Illustrator is not made for multi-page documents and will cause you or future designers headaches. I know, I've had those headaches and had to recreate files properly from scratch before I could work with them.

Just so you know:

- **Adobe Illustrator** is for logo design and illustrations and single-page documents like flyers and posters. Work is 'vector-based' so you can scale it up without any loss of quality.

- **Adobe Photoshop** is for digital manipulation of photographs or images. The 'rasterised' or 'bitmap' images are made of pixels or 'dots'. The resolution (quality of image) is fixed, so the image will blur as it scales up.

- **Adobe InDesign** is a typesetting and layout tool for single or multipage documents like brochures, magazines, books and e-books.

One final little tip: before I engage with a potential partner, I like to check their attention to detail with an innocuous but clear instruction, e.g. 'Please send examples of your work to...' and I give a specific email address (not mine). If they then email me directly, they've not shown an ability to follow a simple brief.

Now that you know how to go about finding your designer, let's have a look at some colour specifications and printing techniques so you can impress them with your knowledge and know how to ask for what you want with confidence and clarity.

Colour Specifications

'Any customer can have a car painted any colour that he wants so long as it is black.'

Henry Ford

There are countless colours, and a surprising number of colour specifications for each of them, so specifying the right ones for your brand can be quite confusing, unless you are Henry Ford. This guide will help you understand your designer when they start talking Pantone, CMYK, spot, process, RGB, HEX or HTML. The first term is a universal colour system, the next three are for print and the last three are for digital colour reproduction.

Pantone: Let's start off with the most well-known. The Pantone Matching System (PMS) is a standard colour specification used by designers and printers worldwide. There are many Pantone swatch books, with new, updated colours every year and there is even a Color Bridge book to match colours across print and online platforms. Pantone's global monopoly means each book costs a fortune to buy, but your printer or designer should have ones you can look at.

A Pantone colour specification is made up of three to six numbers and then a letter, C (coated) U (uncoated) for a spot colour, or CP and UP for a process colour printed on coated or uncoated paper (I'll explain these terms in the Paper Specifications chapter), e.g. Pantone 1350 CP. There are online 'Pantone to CMYK' or 'CMYK to RGB' converters which will also give you colour values, but I've found that different websites give different results, so I always stick to Pantone books as the industry standard.

The idea with Pantone is that you can achieve consistency whichever platform you appear on in the world (printed or online). The reality is, frustratingly, that even print colours can vary quite a lot. This can happen for a variety of different reasons

- Different paper stock (coated, uncoated, the paper base colour) will make the inks look different. Pantone supplies uncoated and coated colour swatches to show the effect of printing the same colours on different papers. The same Pantone red on uncoated paper will look more subdued and duller as the ink is absorbed and 'sinks' into the paper. The Pantone red on coated or gloss paper will look brighter, crisper and more intense as the ink 'sits' on the coating.

- Different makes of printing machines being calibrated differently by different printers (and human error).

- Different printing finishes, e.g. a laminated coating will cause the colour to look slightly different from a print job that isn't laminated (I'll explain these in the 'Special Finishes' chapter).

And that's before we even start looking at digital media (we'll look at screen colour reproduction in a bit). My advice? Find a good printer and stick with them. Always use the same paper stock and finish. And always ask for a printed test 'proof' before you do the full print run to make sure your print colours are as expected and so your designer can adjust anything if need be.

My trusty Pantone swatch book is always close at hand

Print colour reproduction

Process colours are the four CMYK colours (like the cartridges in a domestic colour printer: cyan, magenta, yellow and black – the K stands for 'key' colour). The inks print over the top of each other in a dot pattern to create all other colours.

Also called 'full-colour' or 'four-colour' printing, process colours can be achieved through digital or 'litho' printing (explained later in this chapter). It doesn't cost any more to print one or a thousand colours using process colours as all the colours are made up of four coloured inks.

Spot colours are like Dulux paints, where each individual ink colour is mixed specifically for your job. They include those you cannot reproduce in CMYK, e.g. super-bright greens and oranges, neons, fluorescents and metallics. These colours are impossible to achieve digitally and not all printers can cope with them. Every spot colour you add costs more as it's another colour to mix and another 'pass' of the paper through the print machine.

Most of our clients have no need for spot-colour logos, so my company only provides these on request, e.g. for merchandise with two colours or more. If you are producing merchandise printed with only one colour, just supply your black logo and your printer can use that as artwork to print any spot colour you choose.

Your designer will need to set your finished print artwork up differently for process or spot-colour printing, so be sure everyone knows how it is going to be printed before the artwork is completed. Note that most Pantone process colours are slightly different to their equivalent Pantone spot colour because they are created in two different ways. If you are going to use both print methods in your branding, you and your designer should choose Pantone specifications with a close match across both swatches.

Online colour reproduction

Online specifications take two main forms:

- RGB codes are used by designers to denote onscreen colours. Red, green and blue are the colours of the light diodes in a screen. The numbers 0–225 denote how brightly each light is shining. RGB 0,0,0 is black (no light), 225, 225, 225 is white (full brightness), 135, 75, 149 is a lovely purple.

- HEX or HTML codes are used by coders in programming, each combination of numbers and letters denoting a specific colour. HEX #000000 is black, #FFFFFF is white, #874B95 is that same purple.

As a business owner, you only need to understand that any artwork you view on screen will not look the same when printed. Printed inks work in the opposite way to lit screen diodes. Printing all the CMYK inks at maximum intensity will give you a rich, deep black but when RGB lights are all shining at maximum intensity, they emit a bright white light. In addition, digital devices all have varying colour intensity, brightness and contrast settings and some can show a wider range of colours.

As long as you have colour consistency across all your printed collateral (your business cards, brochures, flyers, posters, signage, etc) and colour consistency across all your online materials (your website, social ads, advertising banners, etc), you'll be fine. Take comfort in the fact that no one will ever hold your business card and pull you up on not having the exact colour match on your website.

Printing techniques

There are lots of methods of printing, but as an entrepreneur, you will generally be looking at these two options: digital or 'litho'.

Digital printing

Digital printing is the most common form of printing. Fast and cheap, digital printing works either as a laser or inkjet printer, mixing up the four process CMYK inks to produce most colours under the sun (with the aforementioned notable exceptions). Most commercial books, magazines, newspapers, newsletters, labels, stationery, menus and brochures are printed digitally. The costs scale up proportionally to your print run, but there is usually no minimum print run.

Digital printing does mean you may be limited on choices of what to print on as thicker weights of paper and card won't feed through the machine.

Offset lithography printing

'Litho' is the traditional way of printing, with proper printing presses. Metal plates have your design etched into them and rubber rollers transfer wet ink from the metal plates on to the paper. This method can print on any flat surface – smooth brochures or rough fabric bags – and you are not restricted by thickness. The wet ink takes longer to dry, so litho is not suitable for any last-minute jobs.

Litho can be a four-colour CMYK process (one plate for each colour), but its main advantage is for printing special spot colours not achievable with digital, including neons and metallics. Colours with litho are much richer and the print quality feels more expensive, so this is great for a luxury and high-end look (although as digital is increasing in quality, this is becoming less of an issue).

Litho is more expensive to set up, but gets cheaper the more you print, so as long as the artwork stays the same, subsequent print runs won't cost as much. There does come a tipping point where litho may work out the same or more cost-effective on larger print runs, so do check with your printer.

Other print methods

You are less likely to use these, but it's good to know they exist, just in case:

- **Large format** – a continuous roll of paper is used rather than individual sheets for large, flat print items, like posters, vinyl banners, advertising boards, wallpaper, wall or floor graphics.

- **Flexography** – for packaging, labels and repeat patterns. This allows you to print large runs at high speed on paper, cellophane, plastic and metallic film, e.g. for wallpaper or branded gift wrap.

- **Screen printing** – for fabric, paper, metal or plastic promotional items including t-shirts, notebooks, baseball caps, pens and posters. Best for bulk printing because of set-up costs.

- **LED UV printing** – a more recent form of printing. UV lights dry and 'set' the inks more quickly, allowing more intense, crisp colours as the ink has less time to 'sink' into the paper.

- **Letterpress printing** – dating back to the 15th century, this is the traditional form of printing. Individual letters are made from metal or wooden blocks and put together to make words. Metal type was used for newspapers and books, wooden ones for larger format printing like posters. Letterpress is still used for handmade, decorative and vintage effects.

- **Engraving** – metal plates are etched with a recessed image, creating a raised ink effect on printing. Great for business cards and invitations.

- **3D printing** – computer aided design (CAD) specialists can create branded promotional items 'printed' in microscopic layers of 3D plastic.

Now we know how we're going to print and what colours we're going to use, it's time to have a look at what we're going to print on.

Paper Specifications

'Look at that subtle off-white colouring - the tasteful thickness of it. Oh my God, it even has a watermark.'

Patrick Bateman, American Psycho

You can print pretty much any design on any paper. Your high-street print-copy shop will probably have a limited range of paper weights and finishes, so seek out a proper printer (with traditional printing presses) and prepare to be inspired.

Most skilled printers will 'geek out' talking paper and print all day, and they'll love that you are showing an interest. You'll be able to look through and, more importantly, feel hundreds of paper samples in a myriad of colours, textures and finishes, made out of trees, recycled fabrics, leaves or grasses and incorporating seeds, flowers, coffee grounds. In India, you can even get paper made from elephant dung.

The right paper for your brand

Go back to your Visualise and Inner Brand work. Is your brand high-end and luxurious? Natural and earthy? Corporate and professional? Your paper choices can really help reinforce your brand values and personality. For example:

- If your company sells organic or natural remedies, you may wish to use recycled papers

- A financial client will probably choose to go for a smooth, coated white paper to convey crisp professionalism

- A high-end, luxury brand may have a brochure cover made from a rich-coloured or textured card

Paper finishes

Paper finishes broadly fall into two camps – coated or uncoated. They look and feel different and colours will print differently on them.

Uncoated paper: All paper starts off as uncoated. It may feel slightly less smooth or more textured to the touch than coated paper and is more absorbent so the inks sink in. This gives a softer look to the finished item as the colours end up more muted. Uncoated paper is ideal for handmade, artisanal, earthy, natural, organic, healthy or even retro brands, but is not good for when crisp detail is needed, e.g. fine lines, intricate artwork, technical drawings or detailed photography. Uncoated stock is best for anything that might be written on, e.g. workbook pages or forms.

Coated paper is made by pressing a layer of clay and caulk into the grain of uncoated paper to 'fill in' the microscopic rough terrain and smooth the surface. It feels much smoother and inks sit on top of the paper rather than sinking in, so the colours end up much brighter and crisper. Coated paper is much better for reproducing fine lines and detail. If your brand is polished, high-end, professional, corporate or modern, choose coated paper. Coated paper comes in matt, silk or gloss. Which one you choose all boils down to personal taste and the effect you're going for.

Don't just limit your thinking to smooth, white paper. A different colour or finish could say more about your brand and really help you stand out from the competition

Personally, I think a matt or silk finish looks more understated, quietly classy. Really glossy finishes can look a bit flashy or cheap (especially on thinner stocks), but some nationalities and cultures prefer a glossy finish, so do consider your market – and, of course, the context. A heavier weight gloss paper is ideal for luxury brands or anywhere the photography needs to sing. Matt and silk finishes have less light reflecting off them so are better for anything with copy that needs to be read – i.e. most brochures.

Don't forget that the same colour specifications will print differently on an uncoated or coated paper. For consistency, make sure that all your marketing collateral is printed on the same colour and finish of paper stock (i.e. don't mix a brilliant white coated business card with an off-white uncoated letterhead).

Paper weights

Paper or card weights are measured in grams per square metre (gsm). Bigger numbers mean heavier – and usually thicker – stock. I say 'usually' as the same weight of paper in an uncoated finish may look and feel thicker than in a coated finish, as coated papers get compressed and made thinner in the coating process.

Don't skimp on your paper choice. A cheap or thin stock will reflect badly on the perceived quality of your company. A thick stock will feel more substantial and higher quality than a brochure printed on flimsier stock, but thicker stock is not always better. There are practicalities to take into consideration. Although you could print a poster on thick card, it may be too heavy and fall off the wall. The thickest stock digital printers can handle is 350–400gsm, so that will also limit your choices. Ask your designer or printer to show you existing paper samples and examples of work to help you make up your mind.

Recommendations on paper weights

Here are my recommendations based on the items I'm asked for the most. Don't just go by numbers and what I say, though. Print is your brand made tangible and real – more lasting and tactile than any digital assets – so speak to your designer and printer, and check real-life samples to make sure whatever paper you choose feels right for your brand.

Brochures: for up to twenty-four pages, you can use anything between 170gsm–300gsm (the heavier weights are for the cover). I like using a heavier stock for the cover to give a quality feel, but if it's used throughout, the brochure might keep springing open, so go for a lighter weight on the inside pages. Ask your printer to create a blank dummy brochure in your chosen paper(s) so you can handle and feel the weight of the brochure before you make your final choice.

Business cards are generally 350gsm–450gsm. Your business card is often the first touchpoint with a potential client, so it's got to look and feel good. Try a Google image search (e.g. 'cool business cards') or check Pinterest to get some inspiration. Save your favourites to your mood board and discuss them with your designer. A too-thin card feels cheap and does not imply a quality business. For digital printing, the heaviest stock tends to be 400gsm so if you want a thicker business card, you will need to go litho or have more than one layer of card stuck together. I guess that's why it's not just American psychos who are impressed by a thick business card, especially one with special finishes like embossing, foils or special inks. A 500gsm card is impressive because you've clearly spent more on it.

Folders tend to use 350gsm–400gsm. Speak to your printer and make sure what you choose is fit for your particular purpose. You need it to be strong and sturdy enough to hold other brochures, flyers, proposals or papers. Ask for a blank dummy again or a sample of a similar one they've produced for another job. (Tip: if you use a folder shape they've produced before you may be able to save some money on production.)

Environmental considerations

If you and your brand care about the planet, here are a few further considerations and options.

100% recycled paper is made entirely from other paper and no additional trees are killed in the making of it. Recycled paper may also be made from fabrics or incorporate other materials. You may choose a recycled paper if you want a more earthy, natural, homemade or tactile feel.

Be aware that recycled paper tends to be off-white rather than pristine white because manufacturers generally don't use bleach or other potentially harmful chemicals in their processes.

FSC-accredited paper may be fully or partly recycled, but any virgin pulp comes from 'responsibly sourced timber and timber products', which means there is no harm done to forests, communities and wildlife. Use of this paper allows you to put the FSC logo on your marketing materials.

Reducing ink coverage on your designs makes the paper more recyclable at the end of its life.

Laminating your job means you can't recycle the paper at the end of its life as it adds a thin layer of plastic onto it.

My company has a partnership with a printer, Calvert's in London, that works only with recycled and FSC papers. This company also prints with water-soluble vegetable-based inks (traditional inks are petroleum-based), which are better for the environment. Of course, saving the planet does come with a price – for now. But if you wish to consider more eco-friendly choices, ask your designer or printer for their recommendations.

Special Finishes

'While adding the finishing touches to a painting might appear insignificant, it is much harder to do than one might suppose.'

Claude Monet, Impressionist artist

Whilst not seen as essential, like Monet's last few dabs of paint on his masterpiece, special finishes add an extra *je ne sais quoi* to your printed matter. These are often overlooked because of the cost but if you want your print – especially 'first impression' items like your business cards, brochures or invitations – to have more impact, then they are worth consideration.

Special finishes are a great way to elevate your visibility in the marketplace, position your brand as a class act and make you that touch more memorable. Perhaps this overview of different special finishes will inspire you to try something new.

Laminates: Gloss, matt, silk or soft-touch laminate (often shortened to 'lam' by printers and designers) is a commonplace finishing technique. Laminate is a thin, clear plasticised coating layered on top of the print job to seal the ink and give it a smoother texture. The finish makes the product seem more luxurious as it makes the paper fractionally thicker and protects the ink from being scratched or transferring. It is also slightly stain/water-repellent so great for things that get handled a lot, e.g. menus. Ask your printer about soft-touch laminate – it's more expensive, but just *so* tactile. One of my clients chose this and we couldn't stop stroking her business cards!

Note that lamination will make your printed material impossible to recycle at the end of its life, but it will also prolong its life.

Special inks: Colours that are not achievable through the CMYK printing process need to be printed as a special spot-colour ink, e.g. Day-Glo or neon colours, UV-sensitive or metallic inks. Metallic inks (right) are a beautiful way to get a luxurious soft shimmer rather than a shine and they come in many colours – ask your printer or designer. You can print special inks alongside any CMYK print run, as we did on the reverse of these business cards.

Spot UV ink printed like an additional spot colour on top of your normal print job adds a pop of gloss to highlight a part of the design, a logo or image, so it catches your eye in the light. This technique adds graphic interest and can look really luxurious. A spot UV can be paired with a matt laminate on the other areas of the page for even more visual and textural contrast.

Foil blocking (or hot foil stamping): One of the oldest print techniques (left). The ancient Egyptians used to beat thin sheets of gold leaf into their papyrus paper and old leather-bound books had their titles foiled-stamped into the covers and spines. Gold leaf is obviously super-expensive, so by the 20th century, different coloured foils had been introduced.

Foil blocking is used to give a high-shine finish over a small area for lettering or images on business cards, brochures and invitations. The metal die is made to your design, heated and used to press the foils into the paper. These can give a luxurious look to your branding, but the caveat is that if the design itself isn't high-end, then this technique can look tacky, flashy, showy or clichéd. You can now get foils in shiny or matt, golds, silvers, bronzes, holographics, pearlescents, pastels, brights, whites and even semi-transparent finishes. Ask your printer or designer for inspiration.

Edge painting/foiling: This is when the edges of the paper (in a book, journal, invitation or business card) are given a coloured or foil edge. Quite a few of my clients have gone for this effect, and it really is a lovely way of catching the eye as you hand your card over. Emily Bal, a confidence coach, said she gets 'exactly the reaction she was hoping for' every time she hands over one of her cards with its gorgeous rose-gold foil edging.

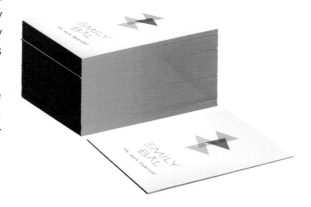

Another way to get colour on the edge of your business card, although with a slightly different effect, is by your printer sandwiching coloured card between two other sheets of card. Sites like www.moo.com offer this effect in a small range of colours.

Case study: Jo Baldwin Trott

Jo is a personal brand consultant. Ironically, when we met, she was feeling stuck, in part because she felt embarrassed to hand out her business cards. They were very 'girly', dated and busy, totally at odds with Jo's target market of innovative and ambitious entrepreneurs.

Jo needed to stand out as a leader in her industry, but also to reflect her personality – a bit rock-chick, bold, straight-talking, not afraid to make an impact. We chose a typographic solution for her long name; a cool, minimalistic font with a hint of Soho's neon lettering. Her new strapline, 'Rock your Personal Brand' now clearly states her brand promise. Jo loves colour, so we chose her favourite teal to make it brilliantly 'her'.

With her Facebook, Twitter, Instagram, website, email and mobile info, her cards ould easily look a mess again. But then I had a thought.

'There's no other Jo Baldwin Trott in the world, is there? We could just put your name on, nothing else!'

That sounded crazy to Jo till I pointed out that nowadays, people just Google you or connect with you on LinkedIn once you hand them your card anyway. So Jo's cards had her name/logo on one side, with a teal reverse. No details, just a silver foil edge for a luxurious touch.

Jo loves her new branding and the reaction her cards get.

'They are a real conversation starter. A bit "Marmite" for some, but it's such a bold, confident statement. Memorable. Makes an impact. I was so embarrassed before and now I feel proud. They are just so me. I finally feel I can really drive the business forward.'

JO BALDWIN TROTT
ROCK YOUR PERSONAL BRAND

Before (left) and after (above)
From top, L-R: logo, social media icon and her show-stopper business cards with the special finish of silver foil edging.

This transformative rebrand ended up with Jo saying she 'felt a big shift and emotional change' - so much so she changed other areas of her life directly afterwards, including joining a band as lead singer!

Die-cuts stamp irregular shapes or holes out of paper or card using a metal die (blade). Die-cutting is expensive to set up as the printer needs to create a bespoke metal die first, but you can get some super-cool effects like having an image peeking through holes in a brochure cover or a business card with a wavy edge. Die-cutting is also used to create the irregular flat shapes needed (with flaps and slits) for fold-up document wallets, folders and boxes. Once you've had your die made for you, subsequent print runs will be considerably cheaper – or ask your printer and you can save money if you choose a previously-created die.

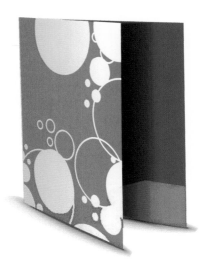

Embossing/Debossing: Embossing gives a raised profile to your design, whilst for debossing, the design is recessed into the paper. A bespoke metal die is used to 'impress' images or lettering into the card or paper. Often combined with other print techniques or special finishes, e.g. engraving or foiling, these processes will give your branding a tactile, luxurious 3D effect – helping you to literally stand out. It's also a delightfully eco-friendly method of printing, the reduced ink coverage making the paper much easier to recycle at the end of its life.

Jargon Buster

'Our business is infested with idiots who try to impress using pretentious jargon.'

David Ogilvy, 'Father of Advertising', founder of Ogilvy & Mather

A plague not just restricted to the advertising industry, I have observed designers, printers and developers all using technical-speak and confusing jargon to bamboozle their clients into submission or justify their fees with their superior knowledge. This chapter is your secret weapon!

Words in italics are defined elsewhere in the list.

Ascender - the upstroke of a letter above the *x-height*, e.g. for b or d.

Bad break - when a word breaks awkwardly over two lines. I include splitting a brand or person's name over two lines as a bad break. Fix these by tweaking the copy or your designer can slightly alter the line length by *tracking* it up or down.

Baseline - imaginary lines that the text sits on. Pictures and graphics when they sit parallel with text baselines, make the layout look more polished.

Binding - method of holding pieces of paper together to form a document. There are several methods of binding, usually led by the thickness, the function of the document and budget:

- **Saddle-stitch** - the most common professional binding procedure, which looks like metal staples down the middle of your document. Cheap, quick and easy.

- **Loop-stitch:** another wire-binding method, but the wires make little loops on the outside of the spine for collating several documents in a bigger file.

- **Stab (or side) stitch:** scarily named, this is where the document is 'stabbed' with the wire from the front of the brochure through the whole thickness of the document and closed up at the back. A covering is usually added to hide the wires afterwards.

- **Sewn-binding:** like saddle stitching, but using thread to sew all the pages together down the middle. A lot more expensive and not used as widely.

- **Tape-binding:** where the pages are stitched together and an adhesive tape is then wrapped tightly round the spine.

- **Perfect-binding:** used for paperbacks and *case-binding* for hardback books. Sections of grouped pages are sewn together and then glued inside the cover for a paperback or to the end papers in a hardback.

- **Plastic-grip binding:** where a length of plastic grips the entire edge of the paper, and comb or spiral binding, as seen on notepads and calendars. Both can be DIY or produced in copy-shops, so they're great for customised documents.

Bitmap – a photograph or other image made up of pixels or 'dots'. Can be *JPEG, TIFF, GIF* or *PNG* formats. The opposite of *vector* images, bitmaps don't scale up without loss of clarity, so files need to be used at the correct resolution for the intended size.

Bleed – an extra 3–5mm of colour or image extending beyond the finished artwork. This allows a small margin of error to make sure the design goes right to the edge of the page.

CMYK – the four colours of the four-colour print process: cyan, magenta, yellow and black (K stands for 'key colour').

Coated – *uncoated* paper that has a fine layer of caulk (chalk powder) pressed into it to smooth the grain. Ink printed on coated paper sits more crisply and looks more vivid than on uncoated paper.

Collateral – the collective name for all your marketing assets, e.g. business cards, brochures, flyers, website…

Compressed – description for a file that is made smaller, so it's easy to transfer or store. Can also be called a 'zipped' file, especially useful if there are several files within a file.

Copy – the written word in your marketing *collateral*.

Coverage – the area of ink printed on a page. A typical page of printed text has about 5% coverage, whereas a brochure cover may have up to 100% coverage. Less coverage means the paper is easier to recycle, more coverage takes jobs longer to dry.

Crop marks – or trims – the little lines at the corners of print-ready artwork, guiding the printer when they crop the finished piece. Important parts of the design or copy should stay at least a few millimetres in from the crops.

Cut-outs – when you remove the background of a photographic image and isolate one element for use in a design. Also a term used for holes punched into a piece of paper by *die-cutting*.

Deckle edge – a torn-edge effect.

Descender – the down stroke of a letter that drops below the *baseline*, e.g. for 'g' or 'y'.

Die-cut – how irregular shapes are cut out of paper or card using a metal die blade, which punches the shape out. Used to create folders, packaging or special effects like a peephole on a brochure cover.

DPI (dots per inch) – a measure of the quality or resolution of an image, literally the amount of 'dots' in an area of the image an inch-square. 300 DPI is the minimum recommended print resolution, 72 DPI for web.

Dummy – a folded and made-up blank sample brochure or package in your chosen paper stock so you can see what it feels like.

Dummy copy or 'lorem ipsum' – copy which designers may use in initial visuals. My university tutor used to call it Pig Latin, but apparently that's a different thing.

Duotone – an effect when an image is printed in only two colours instead of the usual four.

Emboss – when a design is impressed into the paper from the reverse side, raising the image or text up from the front surface of the paper. Debossing is the opposite, when the image is pressed down into the paper.

EPS (Encapsulated PostScript) – a file format. Can be *vector* or *bitmapped*.

Extenders – are *ascenders* and *descenders*, the bits that stick out beyond the *x-height* of a line of copy, e.g. the upstroke of an h or t and the downstroke of a y or j.

Feathering – softening the edge of an image in Photoshop. Useful for cut-out images, e.g. around a person's hair, where accurate cropping is difficult.

Flexography – a form of printing using rubber printing plates for impervious materials, e.g. plastic bags, branded water bottles.

Foil blocking or stamping – a special finish where metallic foil is bonded on to the paper with a hot metal die for a luxury effect on text or images.

Full-colour – also process-colour or four-colour printing uses the four *CMYK* inks to make up all the colours. May be digital or litho printing.

Gatefold – also, confusingly, called a double gatefold. A brochure fold that creates two flaps that meet in the middle but do not overlap.

GIF (graphics interchange format) – a file format used for online and moving images. Low resolution and unsuitable for printing.

Gloss paper – a *coated* paper with a sheen or shine.

Gradient – a gradual transition from one colour to another or a colour fading out to white. Can give a 3D or 'shading' effect.

Grain – the direction the fibres lie in a piece of paper. Folding paper works better if you fold in the same direction as the grain. If it's folded against the grain, this can cause the ink to crack.

Greyscale – artwork or an image made of different percentages of black ink to create various shades of grey, as in newsprint or photocopies.

Grid – an invisible guide used throughout a document or website to anchor and align design elements. Keeps things looking uniform and helps the reader's navigation.

gsm (grams per square metre) – a measure of the weight of paper or card stock per square metre. A higher gsm generally means a thicker stock.

Gutter – the inner margin of a *spread*. Also the gaps between columns of type, for which 6–7mm seems to work almost universally, for some reason.

Halftone – when the image has been converted into dots for printing. Blown up halftone images give an edgy effect, a bit like a Lichtenstein painting.

JPEG or JPG (joint photographic experts' group) – a *bitmap* file format, suitable for online and print, depending on *resolution*. A JPEG/JPG image does not scale up without blurring.

Kerning – adjustments made to visually equalise the white space between individual letters, a precision art form but a vital element of professional typography usually reserved for logos or headings.

Laminate – a thin plasticised coating applied to a print job to seal the print and make the finished items more durable and less prone to scratches, but also less able to be recycled. Comes in matt, silk and gloss finishes.

Leading – the space between lines of text. The term comes from ye olden days and refers to the thin strips of lead wedged between lines of metal type. Generally, the leading (or line spacing) should be a couple of point sizes bigger than the copy size for good legibility (e.g. 12pt copy should be leaded by 14pts). Too little or too much leading interferes with legibility.

Letterpress – a traditional printing method with letters moulded out of metal or carved out of wood.

Logotype – the typeface(s) used for a logo.

Matt – a finish of paper. Can be *coated* or *uncoated*.

Margins – white space left and right of elements on a page. Should stay constant throughout a document. Large margins feel more luxurious as they give more white space. Web developers call margins *padding*.

Monotone – or mono – printing in just one colour. The default colour for mono printing is black, but it doesn't have to be.

Offset lithography – a method of printing also known as litho or offset.

Optimisation – when a file is adjusted to aid retrieval, storage or execution, e.g. a high-resolution image should be optimised (made smaller) for web usage to help the site load faster.

Orphan – the first line of a paragraph set as the last line of a page or column, separated from the rest of its paragraph. Avoid these by editing the copy or asking the designer to adjust the word-breaks or *tracking*. See also *Widow*.

Out-of-register – out-of-fit or out. When one or more of the colours on your finished job has slipped and not printed where it should be.

Outlined – when type in a design is turned into non-editable *vector* shapes. Your logo should be outlined to make sure it stays stable regardless of whether people have the fonts on their systems.

Padding – the web equivalent of *margins*. Plenty of padding left and right of copy on a website makes it look more elegant and easier to read.

Pagination (or paging) – used by designers to mean the number of pages in a document, but actually means adding page numbers to a document.

Pantone Matching System (PMS) – a universal industry standard for print colour matching. Pantone references for your brand colours should keep your collateral looking consistent.

PDF (portable document format) – a stable file format that allows documents to be shared and viewed across different platforms without any loss of formatting, regardless of software or hardware.

PNG (portable network graphics) – a file format for online usage which allows a transparent background. Useful for overlaying logos on images or coloured backgrounds.

pp (printed page) – a 2pp flyer will have two sides printed. A 12pp brochure has twelve printed pages (usually made out of three folded pieces of paper).

PPI (pixels per inch) – an onscreen measure of *resolution*, like print's *DPI*.

Proof – a way of checking your design before it is printed. This can be a digital *PDF* proof to check layout and *copy* or a physical printed proof to check colour reproduction on your chosen paper *stock*. A printed proof also helps you spot any errors/improvements needed in the layout or *copy*. I highly recommend allowing time for and not skipping this important stage.

pt or point size – a term used to define size of type in print.

Rasterised – another word for *bitmap*

Registration – when print colours and elements line up exactly. This is especially important on jobs like business cards where a small discrepancy can make a huge difference. If the front-to-back registration is out, the finished print job will look terrible.

Resolution ('res') – a measure of the quality of an image. Web images can be low resolution (typically 72 *DPI*) and high resolution. Print images have to be 300 DPI at 100% size of reproduction to print clearly. You can downgrade a high-res image for web, but you can't upgrade a low-res web image for print. This is why an image off the internet will not usually print well.

Responsive – a website that automatically resizes and reconfigures its layout to best fit each device it is seen on. Most websites these days are responsive.

RGB – screen colours made up of red, green and blue lights.

Rich black – printing black over large areas can look a bit ashy if you only use the black ink (K). A rich black is made up of layering all the *CMYK* colours to make a much more intense shade with better coverage. Not for text.

Roll-fold (C-fold) – a way of folding an A4 piece of paper in on itself into thirds to create a leaflet.

Scope-creep – when a brief grows arms and legs, morphs and gets bigger as it progresses, causing the job to go on longer than it needs to, rising costs and frustration all round.

Self-cover – when a brochure or booklet cover is the same stock as the inner pages.

Serif and sans-serif (sans) – styles of font. Serifs have the little feet on the ends of the letters, sans-serifs don't. See 'Image' chapter.

Set-off – when a colour from one page rubs off on to the next page, a common problem with high-*coverage* print jobs. A *laminate* coating can seal the ink and stop this happening.

SEO (search engine optimisation) – a dark art which allows you to get found on search engines by potential customers. Constantly changing your website copy – e.g. by adding blogs regularly – will help maintain your SEO. SEO is not a static thing, so you do need to keep working at it.

Silk – a coated finish of paper, between *matt* and *gloss* in appearance.

Special finishes – additional effects on a print job. See Techy Stuff.

Spread – facing pages in a document, typically a left and right hand page, unless it's a *gatefold* brochure.

Spot colour – specific colours mixed to a *Pantone* reference.

Stock – a designer/printer term for paper.

SVG (scaleable vector graphics) – an online *vector* format of an image which is scaleable without loss of quality.

TIFF (tagged image file format) – a *bitmap* file format where no compression of file size is used. Useful for large format printing, e.g. posters or billboards which need huge images.

Tint – printing a percentage of a colour. A colour used at 100%, 50% and 10% tints will give you three shades of the same colour.

Tracking – a method for your designer to subtly lengthen or shorten a line in copy to adjust *widows*, *orphans* or weird word-breaks. Tracking copy shouldn't really be done more than 1–2% so the change in letter and word spacing stays imperceptible. Tracking is also used in logo design to space all the letters out more or crunch them closer together for graphic effect. *Kerning* is different as this is about adjusting individual letter spacing.

Uncoated – paper finish which means the ink sinks into the paper and gives a softer, more muted effect than *coated* paper. All papers start off uncoated.

URL (uniform resource locator) – a website address.

UX (user experience) for websites – the functionality and flow of a website; how users will go through it. Good UX makes a website simple to use and the information easy to find.

Vectors – files and graphics that scale infinitely with no loss of quality. *EPS* (print) and *SVG* (web format) files are vectors. The opposite to *bitmaps*.

Vegetable/water-based inks – a more eco-friendly option. Normal printing inks are petroleum or oil-based.

Widow – is the last line of a paragraph set as the first line of a page or column, seen as undesirable in a document (see also *Orphan*).

x-height – the height of a lower-case x, or any letters that don't have *ascenders* or *descenders* (see *extenders*).

Zig-zag (or zed fold) – where the paper is folded into thirds like a letter 'Z' to make a mini brochure.

Conclusion

This brings us to the end of the book. Well done! We've covered so much ground together.

In Part 1, I took you on a journey through the history and importance of branding. We learned the difference between brand, branding and personal branding, identifying the three key problems for entrepreneurs (clarity, resource and visibility) and how these issues affect building your brand in the DoSaySee model. We then looked at how to conduct a branding assessment.

In Part 2, we worked through the six-step VISION process to build a brand with solid foundations:

- **Visualise** – your FABs, your vision, your customer's vision

- **Inner Brand** – your brand values, personality and voice

- **Stand Out** – your competitor analysis, other industries and inspiration

- **Image** – the power of type, colour and imagery

- **Outputs** – brand guidelines, tips on brochures and websites

- **Nurture** – looking after your brand, evolving it, protecting it.

In Part 3 I gave you an in-depth exposé on 'the techy stuff' so you can understand colour reproduction, paper types, print techniques and special effects, and finished with a Jargon Buster to help you have more informed discussions with your creatives.

I hope you've enjoyed the read and that I've opened your eyes to the power of branding for your business. At the very least, I hope you will realise that your brand is not your logo!

I hope too that you are feeling all fired up about creating the brand of your dreams to help you gain brand clarity, stand out and supercharge your business growth.

If you've not done so already, don't forget to take our Brand Assets Health Check at www.innervisions-id.com/quiz/.

Bibliography

Boothman, N (2008) *How To Make People Like You In 90 Seconds Or Less.* Toronto: Thomas Allen & Son.

De Soto, D (9th edn. 2017) *Know Your Onions – Graphic Design: How to think like a creative, act like a businessman and design like a God.* Amsterdam: BIS Publications.

Edwards, B (1989) *Drawing on the Right Side of the Brain.* Toronto: Tarcher/ Penguin.

Gannett, A (2018) *The Creative Curve: How to develop the right idea, at the right time.* London: Virgin Digital.

Garfield, S (2010) *Just My Type: A book about fonts.* London: Profile Books.

Gladwell, M (2006) *Blink: The Power of Thinking Without Thinking.* London: Penguin Books.

Kondo, M (2014) *The Life-Changing Magic of Tidying Up: The Japanese art of decluttering and organizing.* Emeryville: Ten Speed Press.

Russell, H (2015) *The Year of Living Danishly.* London: Icon Books.

Truss, L (2003) *Eats, Shoots and Leaves: The zero tolerance approach to punctuation.* London: Profile Books.

Acknowledgements

Thank you to my family, friends and everyone who supported me whilst I was writing this book, especially Andy who kept me fed, watered and motivated whilst I let household duties slide to get this done.

To my wonderful clients who trusted me with their businesses, hopes, dreams and ambitions, and who generously tell others about the work I've done for them; and to everyone who has allowed me to feature them in this book.

To Andrew Priestley who unknowingly kickstarted my business way back when and then, in a beautifully-circular twist, wrote my foreword years later.

To everyone else who has helped me with the business in any shape or form, especially Andy, Jade, Esme, Alexandra and Tim.

To my beta readers and praise-quote givers: Daniel Priestley, Lorna Reeves, Sebastian Bates, Antoinette Oglethorpe, Alexander Seery, Sara Milne Rowe, James White, Tim Pat (whose comment about me on LinkedIn made my day and we are now connected!), Esme Fisher, Jade Staiano and Laura Hurst.

Massive thanks to Lucy McCarraher for her amazing support and kicks up the backside when I wobbled, thinking I couldn't do this; plus Joe Gregory, Kate Latham and Anke Ueberg from Rethink Press, without whom this book would never have existed. I especially appreciate your patience in accommodating my creative vision for this book.

And finally, thanks to Miss Hanlon, my art teacher, without whose early encouragement I would not be doing what I am doing today.

Picture Credits

InnerVisions ID examples and case studies reproduced with client permission.

Other images: p17 Lucky Strike poster reproduced with permission; p25 Rebecca Godfrey photograph © Rebecca Godfrey, by Alex Smutko; p106 GUCCI logo image © Tooykrub/Shutterstock.com; p113 Coca Cola logo image © Rose Carson/Shutterstock.com; Google logo image © rvlsoft/Shutterstock.com; p119 facebook logo image © rvlsoft/Shutterstock.com, pepsi logo image © Allmy/Shutterstock.com, Jo Malone logo image © Gargantiopa/Shutterstock.com, MANCAVE logo reproduced with permission, Microsoft logo image © tanuha2001/Shutterstock.com, Deutsche Bank logo image © rafapress/Shutterstock.com, *The Telegraph* logo image © chrisdorney/Shutterstock.com, YouTube logo image © rvlsoft/Shutterstock.com, iPhone logo image © Narit Jindajamorn/Shutterstock.com; p128 Lorna Reeves photograph © Lex Fleming; p129 Ellie Rich-Poole photograph © John Cassidy, The Headshot Guy; p131 Colin Reeves photograph © Sarah Legge Photography, Michael Coates photograph © Michael Coates, p131 and p221 Sapna Pieroux photographs © Maria Brosnan; p162 Coca Cola cans © The Coca-Cola Company reproduced with permission. All other photographs © Shutterstock. All other images © InnerVisions ID.

The Author

Sapna Pieroux's career has spanned design, marketing, advertising and media sales. She has worked with brands such as Mastercard, Mercedes and Sony Ericsson for companies like Chrysalis, EMAP and the Telegraph Media Group.

Her branding consultancy, InnerVisions ID, helps ambitious impact entrepreneurs and business owners across the globe make a difference. She developed the VISION process to improve understanding and the branding experience between clients and their creatives. This means clearer communication; faster, better outcomes; increased brand clarity and supercharged business growth.

Published in The Huffington Post, and co-author of three best-selling Amazon titles, Sapna is also a brand mentor for national programme Shifts to Success and a business mentor for the Enterprise Hub at the University of West London.

Printed in Great Britain
by Amazon